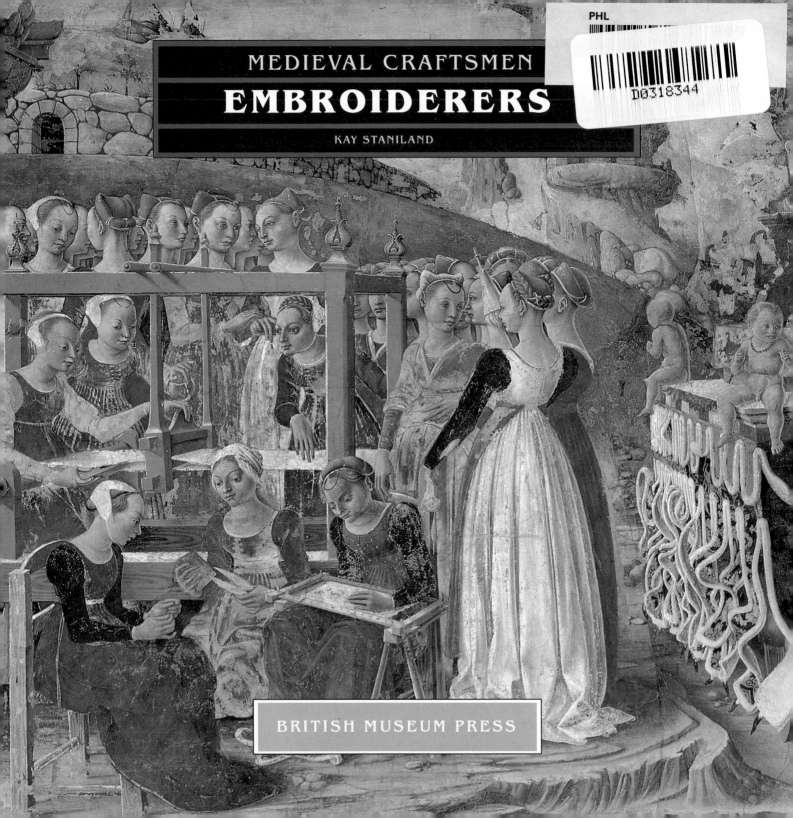

MEDIEVAL CRAFTSMEN
EMBROIDERERS

KAY STANILAND

BRITISH MUSEUM PRESS

For my mother, who encouraged me to embroider in childhood.

© 1991
British Museum Press
3rd impression 1994

Published by
British Museum Press,
a division of
British Museum Publications Ltd,
46 Bloomsbury Street,
London WC1B 3QQ

British Library Cataloguing-
in-Publication Data
Staniland, Kay
    Medieval craftsman:
    embroiderers – (Medieval
    craftsman).
    1. Embroidery, history
    I. Title II. Series
    746.4409

ISBN 0-7141-2051-0

Designed by Roger Davies
Set in Palatino by Southern
Positives and Negatives,
SPAN, Lingfield, Surrey
Printed and bound
in Hong Kong

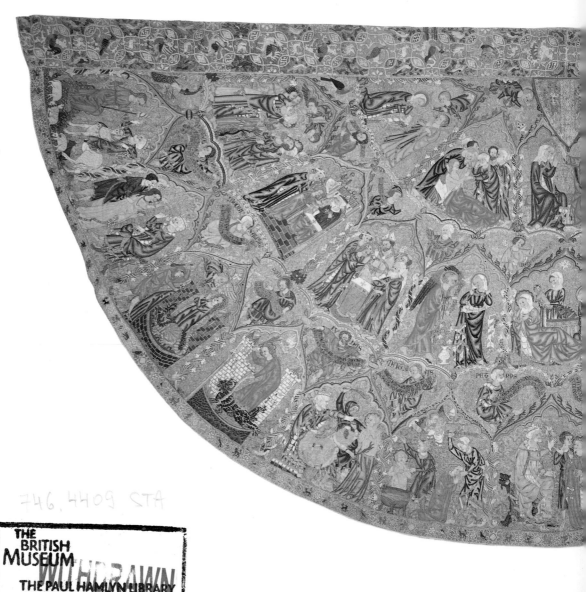

This page The Pienza Cope, given to Pienza Cathedral in 1462 by Pope Pius II (Aeneas Silvio de'Piccolomini 1458–64); it is said to have been brought to Italy and presented to the Pope by Thomas Paleologus, Despot of the Morea. English work of 1315–35. The cope is ornamented with scenes from the lives of the Virgin, St Margaret and St Catherine, in three concentric zones.

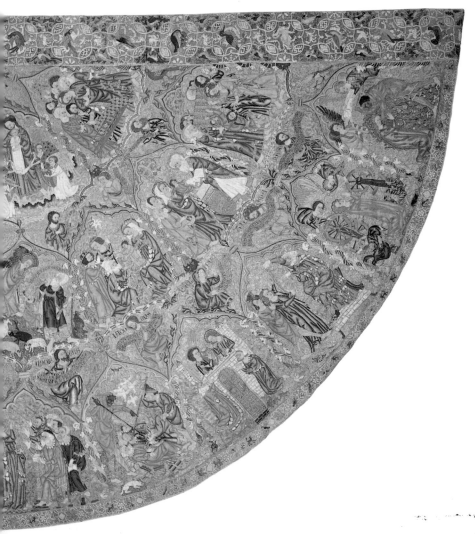

Contents

Introduction 4

1 The Early Embroiderers 7

2 The Guilds 13

3 The Designers 19

4 Production 27

5 Techniques 33

6 The Later Embroiderers 49

7 Patrons 55

Epilogue 62

Glossary 70

Further reading 71

Photographic credits 71

Acknowledgements 71

Index 71

Front cover Craftsmen at work on embroidered hangings. See fig. 24.

Back cover Detail of the Virgin Mary from the Mantle of the Virgin. See fig. 48.

Title page 'The Triumph of Minerva'. See fig. 54.

Introduction

For well over a thousand years embroidery has been a means of adding decoration to clothing, personal accessories and household and church furnishings. Its origins are now lost to us: no-one knows whether this natural development of 'needle and thread' technology arose in one of the ancient civilisations of the Near or Far East, and was gradually spread throughout the known world, or whether the invention was spontaneous and coincidental in several early cultures. At present the latter theory is considered most likely, but there remain many areas of research for textile historians to explore. Archaeological excavations continue to produce new evidence, whilst many older finds have yet to be examined in depth or published.

Whichever theory may eventually be accepted, the evidence in Europe certainly suggests that the concept of adding needleworked decoration to clothing was well established during the Early Bronze Age (1500–500 BC) in Denmark at least; archaeological finds revealing early forms of embroidery elsewhere in Europe belong to the Iron Age (c.500–100 BC). From [1, 2] these insubstantial and fragmentary finds we can deduce only a little about the use and forms of embroidery until the Anglo-Saxon (c.400–1042 AD) and Viking (c.800–1050 AD) periods, when more examples are available. Although textiles normally do not last well, being especially fragile and vulnerable objects, a surprisingly large quantity of embroideries survive from the Middle Ages in Europe to attest the skill and patience of countless craftspeople, both male and female, now almost wholly anonymous through lack of documentation. Like illuminated manuscripts, precious metals and jewellery, sculpture or wall-painting, richly woven or embroidered textiles were much prized and cherished in the Middle Ages, primarily as symbols of wealth, status and power.

Embroidery is the art of applying decoration by needle and thread to the surface of a piece of woven cloth, usually called the 'ground'. It is not an integral part of the weaving process itself, like weaving stripes or checks, or making more complex designs by brocading, or a pile like velvet, all of which are carried out while the cloth is still on the loom. Embroidery is an optional additional decoration worked after the completion of the whole weaving process, including the dyeing and finishing processes. Misuse of terminology has brought about several confusions. For example, tapestry is a form of weaving, but the popularly known Bayeux Tapestry is in fact a large embroidered, [60] not woven, hanging, for it is embroidery carried out on an already-woven ground. Today the word 'tapestry' is also used to refer to cross-stitches worked on a woven canvas ground; in the last century this was usually known as Berlin wool work and again is really an embroidery technique.

Symbols of wealth such as pearls, cameos, enamels, semi-precious and precious stones

1 Decorative stitching on the sleeve of a 'blouse' from the early Bronze Age burial at Skrydstrup, Denmark.

2 Stem stitch embroidery depicting round male faces linked by an interlacing pattern, found in a Viking barrow burial at Mammen, Denmark. Other embroideries found in the burial depict birds, a leopard, a vine and faces, and attest the early popularity of embroidery.

71 appearing in the late 1520s, whilst embroidered samplers were also beginning to proliferate.

In today's consumer-orientated society textiles tend to be very much taken for granted: produced on a massive scale they are then fairly rapidly discarded. Medieval people, however, prized their clothes and furnishings much more highly. Rich cloths, silks, tapestries and em- 3 broideries were vital symbols of wealth and status, second only to precious metals and jewels. They were easily portable and the great demand for rich silks and finely dyed cloths brought radical changes in production and marketing as the Middle Ages progressed. In turn the increasing range of available goods meant that aspirations throughout the social structure could be satisfied, fed by new luxuries and novelties at the upper levels, whilst a lively second-hand market organised the recycling of discarded goods at every level of society.

Ornamentation by embroidery, however, must have been an almost exclusive prerogative of the wealthy ruling classes, certainly in the early Middle Ages. It was a consistently important element in ecclesiastical splendour and many examples of embroidered vestments have survived in church and cathedral treasuries, carefully preserved in specially constructed chests. Magnificent embroideries were an in- contents page, 9, 59 tegral part of medieval international diplomacy both as gifts and as impressive attire for king and pope, prince and prelate alike. Professional embroidery workshops probably existed quite early in the Middle Ages to produce these much-prized possessions, and though little information is now available about these independent workshops, particularly those responsible for the creation of *opus anglicanum*, more is known of the workforces and practices of the royal workshops in London and Paris.

The end of the Middle Ages in Europe is imprecisely defined, Italian influence already being seen in embroidery design in France in the middle years of the fourteenth century just as the final great phase of English medieval embroidery had reached its peak. Indeed, at the end of the century we hear of a Florentine merchant Michiel de Passe, a resident of Avignon who traded in Florentine embroideries to the dukes

were all incorporated into medieval embroideries to provide additional enrichment. 53 Later in the period motifs in solid gold were added too, so much so that the stitchery became merely functional, holding the pearls or orna- 51 ments in place, so that the term embroidery becomes less appropriate.

Many variations of stitches and techniques gradually evolved over the centuries, their countries of origin now unknown, and eventually became part of the whole European repertoire of embroidery stitches, later acquiring individual names. The movement of skilled embroiderers from country to country, attested in the thirteenth century, as well as the transportation of the embroideries themselves, no doubt influenced the dissemination of techniques and styles. Advances in the weaving of rich and decorative silks possibly affected the livelihood of professional embroiderers, but the growing wealth of the merchant classes provided new markets as well as an increasingly domestic aspect to the creation and use of embroidery. 29, 77 Books of printed embroidery designs began

of Burgundy. Perhaps because of the influence of wealthy patronage, Flanders and Italy outstripped all other embroidery centres in the fifteenth century. Growing wealth amongst the merchant classes brought more secular patronage to professional embroiderers, but resulting works have not stood the test of time so well as those of the Church. Patrons increasingly favoured the products of the loom, elaborate gold-enriched velvets and large narrative tapestries, forcing embroiderers to change their techniques and seek new markets.

1 THE EARLY EMBROIDERERS

Embroiderers, in common with their colleagues in the medieval textile trades – carders, spinners, dyers, cloth-weavers, fullers, braid-weavers and tailors – have left little information about themselves in surviving documents for, like most contemporary craftsmen, they worked independently of the large medieval establishments, royal, noble or ecclesiastical, which generated the written records now so helpful to historians. The careful display of their work in the major museums of the world always stimulates curiosity about these shadowy, almost totally anonymous, craftsmen and admiration for their creations.

How much of what survives was produced by professional rather than by amateur embroiderers? How did they acquire their skills? Did they work at home or did they gather in larger workshops to create the more ambitious commissions? How much did they earn? Were they always poor or could they become wealthy?

4 Craftsmen assembling an ecclesiastical vestment. The trestles supporting the work are exactly the same as those shown in use by other craftsmen in this Italian manuscript of *c.*1400.

Who decided the subject matter for the embroideries and who drew up the designs? Who bought or commissioned them, and what did they cost to buy? Were they worked only by women, or were men involved too? So dramatically do the technical skills of the past outshadow anything that can be achieved today, particularly with regard to the scale of what was attempted and the time given to it, that we are naturally prompted to move on to consider these aspects.

Some of the medieval embroidery which survives must certainly be the work of talented amateurs. Archaeological evidence shows something of the antiquity, origins and possibly widespread diffusion of the craft. What has survived in museums and cathedral treasuries tends to give a mistaken impression that embroidery was a luxury item restricted to the wealthy, but these are simply treasured masterpieces carefully preserved through reverence, association or, in some instances, sheer chance. Humbler use of stitching for decorative purposes must have abounded; no great technical mastery is involved in the simpler forms of embroidery and it was almost certainly more widely practised than many now realise. From earliest times, embroidery seems to have enjoyed the rare distinction of being a craft regarded as an acceptable occupation for noble women, and many are the queens accredited with great skills by chroniclers. King Canute (1016–35), for example, is said to have presented altar-cloths worked by his first wife, Aelgifu of Northampton, to the abbeys of Croyland and Romsey; William of Malmesbury recorded that Queen Edith, wife of Edward the Confessor (1042–66), embroidered with her own hands the robes worn by the King at festivals.

In convents, too, embroidery was considered an acceptable occupation as long as it was devoted to worthy ends and did not distract from worship. The chronicler Thomas of Ely recorded that St Etheldreda, Abbess of Ely (d.679), was a skilful craftswoman in gold

embroidery who had offered to St Cuthbert a stole and maniple of fine and magnificent embroidery in gold and precious stones. Indeed, these may have been very similar to the fine gold embroideries later placed in St Cuthbert's tomb. As early as AD 747 an attempt was made to check the tendency, clearly already very prevalent in convents, to spend so many hours in needlework: an ecclesiastical council, held at Clovesho, recommended that instead the reading of books and singing of psalms should receive greater attention. The problem was not so easily resolved, however, for throughout the Middle Ages clerics and commentators were to return to the subject of this distraction from the central purpose of convent life. A balancing view may be found in the approach of the seventh-century Abbess of Bourges Eustadiola who, believing that idleness was the root of all evil, was keen to find work for herself and her nuns through the production of beautiful vestments and altar- and wall-hangings for their church; by this means, she believed, evil would be kept at bay. Already in the ninth century these fine embroideries were highly acceptable and much sought after diplomatic gifts. Thus the distraction continued to be tolerated.

In the eleventh century the lady Aelthelswitha, daughter of King Canute's second wife Queen Aelgiva (Emma) 'rejected marriage and was assigned Coveney, a place near the monastery [of Ely] where', so Thomas of Ely recorded, 'in retirement she devoted herself, with her maids, to gold embroidery. At her own cost and with her own hands, being extremely skilled in the craft, she made a white chasuble'. Church vestments seem to have been the main product of this little workshop, some of which were presented to Ely Cathedral. A beautifully embroidered white headband is later mentioned in an inventory of Ely's possessions as having been made by Aelthelswitha, and is listed among a number of other headbands where the giver, rather than the maker, is specified. The fact that the chronicler bothers to comment on something made 'with her own hands' implies that most of the work was done by, or was expected to be done by, the maids or young girls in Aelthelswitha's charge.

Fine embroidery was not solely confined to convents however, and professionals — those paid to carry out their skills — already existed in the secular working community. It was probably still a somewhat rare and specialised skill, the ability to work with gold thread being especially prized, and the embroideresses were well rewarded. The Domesday Survey contains at least two references to such skilled embroideresses. Aelfgyd held land at Oakley in Buckinghamshire 'which Godric the sheriff granted her [to hold] as long as he was sheriff, on condition of her teaching his daughter embroidery work' whilst Leofgyd held a good estate of moderate size at Knook in Wiltshire because 'she used to make, and still makes, the embroidery of the King and Queen'. At her death in 1083, Matilda, Queen of William the Conqueror, bequeathed to the Church of The Holy Trinity at Caen 'the chasuble which is being embroidered at Winchester by Alderet's wife; the cloak wrought in gold, laid up in my chamber, to make a cope of; . . . and another robe now being embroidered in England'.

The numbers of women skilled in needlecrafts throughout Europe, and beyond, must have

5 *Above* Figure of St Peter from the fragmentary stole of St Cuthbert, worked in England between 909 and 916 at the instigation of Queen Ethelfleda. It is believed that, together with the matching maniple, this was presented to St Cuthbert's shrine at Chester-le-Street in 934 by King Athelstan (924–40).

6 *Right* Detail of the gold background, worked in underside couching, showing a network of circles containing rampant lions and foliate crosses. From an apparel for an alb of English work of 1310–40 showing the Annunciation, Visitation and Nativity.

been increased by the patronage of kings, queens, churchmen and nobles. The equipment needed for embroidery was neither considerable nor expensive: needles, a simple wooden frame and, possibly, a thimble. It was the materials used in the creation of the embroidery – the threads of silk, silver or gold and the silk grounds – which were so expensive, whilst the hours spent by the embroideresses on the larger, more ambitious pieces gradually accumulated, increasing the total cost charged to the patron. Some idea of the time involved can be gleaned from an entry in an account of payments made in 1271 for an altar-frontal for the high altar in Westminster Abbey: 'For the wages of four women working on the aforesaid cloth for $3\frac{3}{4}$ years £36'.

Small embroideries such as bands or or-

phreys, mitres, cushions or purses, could easily be worked upon in a domestic setting and would probably have been the responsibility of a single embroideress. But more space and a larger workforce were needed for the completion of larger objects such as copes or chasubles, altar-cloths, mantles or wall-hangings, for example. Some embroidery workshops seem to have been created especially for this purpose, usually under royal patronage so that the costs of materials, accommodation and wages were assured. Work of this calibre was so specialised and costly that it could only be created under exceptional conditions. Just as in Byzantium, where weaving and embroidery for court use were carried out in the closed and protected situation of special royal workshops, so too in Palermo several centuries later were the mag-

7, 8, 37, 53

7, 8 According to tradition this mitre was given to Kloster Seligenthal in Germany by the Duchess Ludmilla (c.1170–1240). It is of English work of the period 1180–1210, on white silk twill with scenes of the martyrdoms of SS Thomas (*left*) and Stephen (*right*) in underside couching in silver-gilt thread.

nificent and ornate robes and insignia created for the rulers of the Holy Roman Empire. As wealth in society grew and spread, the use of pearls and gemstones in embroideries increased, helping to maintain the visual pre-eminence of its leaders, involving embroiderers in new techniques, expensive outlays on materials and a greater need for secure workshops, and bringing other craftsmen, notably goldsmiths, into closer association with embroiderers.

Of the organisation of these workshops we know virtually nothing, for references in surviving documents usually name only individuals. Mabel of Bury St Edmunds, for example, is one thirteenth-century English embroideress whose name has become synonymous with *opus anglicanum*, despite the fact that we know little about the embroidery she carried out. Her name occurs at least twenty-four times in the household accounts of Henry III (1216–72) in the years 1239 to 1245, during which period she was engaged upon several embroidery projects for the King. For instance in 1239 the royal accounts show that she was working upon a chasuble and an offertory veil; work on the chasuble seems to have continued for the next three years, and payments for gold, pearls, silk and fringe were duly recorded in the accounts. So, too, was the King's command that the value of the chasuble be appraised 'by the sight of discreet men and women with a knowledge of embroidery' to establish Mabel's fee. This appraisal does not appear to have been carried out, for another order was soon issued, and an appraisal requested from the 'better workers of the city of London … such as will speak and know how to speak of such work', and the King emphasised that he needed embroiderers to advise him on the value of the finished work, the cost of materials and Mabel's fee because 'he did not want to offend in this matter nor incur to some extent condemnation of himself.' Mabel also worked on apparels, a stole, a fanon, amice, collar and cuffs for the King, and her last work was an embroidered banner or standard to be hung near the altar in Westminster Abbey.

Between 1245 and 1256 Mabel is absent from the royal records, but in the latter year Henry made a pilgrimage to Bury St Edmunds and whilst there issued the following command: 'Because Mabel of St Edmunds served the King and Queen for a long time in the making of ecclesiastical ornaments … that the same Mabel be given six ells of cloth, appropriate to her [status], and the lining of a robe of rabbit fur'. The gift of warm clothing of this kind was traditional in the royal household and a frequent measure of the King's gratitude for faithful service.

Embroidery historians have frequently cited these references to Mabel of Bury St Edmunds, thus giving her a fame perhaps not altogether justified, while overlooking other embroideresses who also supplied the royal household directly. For instance, in 1253, Maud de Cantuaria (of Canterbury) was paid ten marks (£6 13s. 4d.) for a set of embroidered apparels supplied to the King's half-sister, Alice de Lusignan. In the same year payments of £27 11s. 8d. were made to Maud de Benetleye for sixteen broad and narrow orphreys, and of 64s. to Joan de Woburn for two orphreys.

Henry III is famous as a patron of the arts, and his generosity was prodigious, especially to the Church. To supply the costly ecclesiastical vestments such generosity demanded, he turned to Adam de Basing, a London merchant and mayor in 1251. De Basing has often been incorrectly cited by historians as a London embroiderer, and it has been suggested, though not proved, that he ran embroidery workshops. Most likely he was simply a merchant entrepreneur, a middleman commissioning and buying embroideries, always with stocks of the vestments that rich customers like the King would offer to churches or to favoured visitors or send as presents with ambassadors.

To help the production flow of stock it is possible that de Basing financed London embroiderers by some means. If so, he was certainly investing in a very lively and profitable market. For example, the thirteenth-century Chronicler Matthew Paris noted in his *Chronica Maiorum* for 1246 that at this time 'my Lord Pope' (Innocent IV, 1243–54), having noticed that the ecclesiastical vestments of certain English priests came from England, commanded

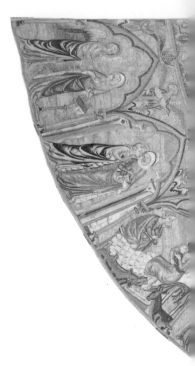

27, 51, 65

9 The Bologna Cope (worked 1315–35) is believed to have belonged to Pope Benedict XI (r.1303–4). Worked in the stitches traditional to *opus anglicanum* it is composed of two concentric rows of cinquefoil arches, the upper row framing scenes of the Passion and Resurrection (the Easter cycle) and the lower row with scenes of the infancy of Christ (the Christmas cycle) terminating with the martyrdom of the most celebrated English saint, Thomas of Canterbury (on 29 December). The narrower upper and lower bands contain the heads of Christ, SS Peter and Paul and other saints. The figure style is related to contemporary paintings at Westminster Abbey. Worn areas in the embroidery reveal that the draughtsman designed various patterns to be worked in the gold background which the embroiderers ignored, making a plain background.

the Cistercian Abbots to supply him with some without delay. 'This command of my Lord Pope', Paris records, 'did not displease the London merchants who traded in these embroideries and sold them at their own price.' Adam de Basing may well have been one of the merchants who benefited from the Pope's lust for these exquisite status symbols.

Furthermore, it is noteworthy that it was the merchants of London whom Paris saw as benefiting, not the embroiderers, though Henry III's prodigality cannot have done other than boost the production of embroidery. It is not surprising, therefore, to find Gregory of London, a gold embroiderer, in the household of Pope Urban IV (1261–4), supported there financially by the Prior and Convent of Bermondsey. It is likely that he was working directly upon embroideries for the Vatican; his annual salary of fifteen marks almost certainly deprived London merchants of a healthy profit.

In the Middle Ages many craft skills were handed down from generation to generation in the same family and many such craft dynasties are attested in the increasing quantity of surviving documents. These can at the very least record the births, marriages and deaths of the craft community, even their misdemeanours, rivalries and conflicts; some documents record the statutes and leading craftsmen of specialist guilds or confraternities. However, despite the quantity of embroidery that was being carried out on a professional basis in London there are regrettably few references to embroiderers in City records. Still, one late thirteenth-century family dynasty has now been researched in some depth since its surname of *Settere* can be shown to be derived from a Middle-English term for embroidery, and craftsmen bearing this surname have occasionally been referred to in

London records: Alexander Settere, for example, who in 1307 received £10 'from Sir Poncius Roandi chaplain to Master William Testa ... in part payment of £40 for an embroidered choir cope bought of the said Alexander, who will well and befittingly complete it of the same breadth around as a certain cord, sealed with the seal of the said Sir Poncius at both ends', a fascinating record of how measurements were agreed and transmitted. A few years later, in 1314, William le Settere and John Heyroun, *settere*, were called upon to value a silk-embroidered cope. The Heyrouns seem to have been another City dynasty of professional embroiderers, probably also carrying out the work we now call *opus anglicanum*. In 1327–8 Johanna Heyroun of London supplied black vestments for use in Edward III's chapel when celebrating the office of the dead; one cannot help concluding that these must relate to the murder of his father Edward II at Berkeley Castle and the subsequent lavish burial service at Gloucester Cathedral. In the same year a Matilda la Settere worked for a short time in the embroidery workshops of the young Edward III. In this way we begin to make contact with individuals in the embroidery community of medieval London, a group of people who created some of the most admired embroideries the world has known.

Payments in 1271 for an altar-frontal in Westminster Abbey (see page 9), made on behalf of Henry III shortly before his death, reveal the great cost and considerable labour expended upon these church embroideries. Gold and silk thread, pearls, enamels, garnets set in gold, and silver plaques, totalled over £220, whilst the labour of four women for $3\frac{3}{4}$ years amounted to an additional £36.

2 THE GUILDS

By the fourteenth century most craftsmen in the capitals of medieval Europe had formed specialist guilds or confraternities with statutes regulating many aspects of their craft; some even appended the names of their craftmembers. In London the embroiderers are believed to have had a guild or confraternity in the fourteenth century, to have drawn up ordinances in the fifteenth century, but to have received their first Charter only in 1561. The embroiderers of Paris did not form a guild until 1471, although we know that they were a well organised and well disciplined craft with statutes dating from 1292 onwards.

The late formalisation of the London and Paris guilds may reflect a change in social, urban or commercial circumstances which required an established central organisation for each community of embroiderers. It is indeed curious that the most outstanding period in the history of English embroidery (1250–1350) should coincide with the time when other craftsmen were coming together to form guilds and confraternities, while in London embroiderers did not yet seem to have felt the need to formalise an organisation that apparently existed informally. Possibly the craft was still predominantly in the hands of women, like the silkwomen and braidweavers who banded together informally to protest when their trades were threatened but do not appear to have belonged to a formal association. The regulations agreed in 1292 by the Paris embroiderers, however, almost certainly reflect something of the attitudes, working methods and conditions of embroiderers in London and other major European cities.

These regulations, approved in 1303 by the then Provost of Paris, Guillaume de Hangest, are published here in full, in translation, the earliest known regulations of any embroiderers in Europe.

1292–1303

'Judgement of Guillaume de Hangest, Provost of Paris, confirming the statutes of the Embroiderers and Embroideresses in twelve articles.

To all who see these letters, Guillaume de Hangest, Governor of the Provostship of Paris, greetings. Let it be known to all that this is agreed and ordained by the whole corporation of embroiderers and embroideresses in the city of Paris. [There follows a list of about two hundred masters and mistresses most of whom reappear in the statute of 1316].

1. Firstly it is ordained that to be an embroiderer or embroideress in Paris a person must know how to practise the craft of embroidery according to the uses and customs, which are as follows:

2. Firstly it is ordained that no man or woman in the said guild may have a male or female apprentice henceforth until the last of those currently retained by them enter their last year of service, counting all defaults.

3. Furthermore no man or woman can henceforth have more than one male or female apprentice together at one time, nor may they take another until either the male or female apprentice enters the last year of his or her service, as stated above.
[This article is a bit obscure, it seems to mean that a master may have two apprentices, but only if one of them is male and the other female; new apprentices can be engaged at the start of the last year of indenture of the existing apprentices, a male to replace the male or a female to replace the female.]

4. Furthermore no guild member, man or woman, can henceforth engage a male or female apprentice for less than eight years' service, whether they have money for this or they have none at all, but they may take them for a longer term as they wish.

5. Furthermore, no man or woman may work at the said craft by candlelight, but only as long as daylight lasts, for work done at night cannot be so well or skilfully done as that done by day.

6. Furthermore, whoever is found working at night will pay a fine of 2 sols, i.e. 12 deniers to the king and 12 deniers to the wardens [gardes] of the guild.

7. Furthermore, no man or woman may work at the said craft on Sundays, on the four feasts days of Our Lady or on the six feasts of the Apostles decreed as fast days, and whoever is found working on any of these days will pay a fine of 2 sols, of which 12 deniers to the king and 12 deniers to the wardens of the guild.

8. Furthermore no man or woman can engage a male or female apprentice unless he or she owns a workshop and unless he or she is a worker at the craft.

9. Furthermore it is ordained that no man or woman guildmember should use gold in their work that costs less than 8 sols the rod for one cannot do embroidery of the

appropriate standard with cheaper material, and whoever contravenes this will pay a fine of 8 sols, 5 sols to the king and 3 sols to the wardens of the guild.

10. Furthermore it is ordained that no man or woman may go to work in the house of anyone who is not a guildmember, since it is unseemly that workers should go to those who know nothing of the craft, and great inconvenience arises from it, since, when masters have contracts for work with rich men, they cannot find their workers and through their fault they cannot fulfil their contracts with the rich men. And whoever goes to work [in a non-guild establishment] will pay a fine of 2 sols, 12 deniers to the king and 12 deniers to the masters.

11. Furthermore it is ordained that anyone doing gold-thread work shall sew with silk.

12. In the above-named guild there will be four qualified people sworn to oversee the ordinances of the guild, whom the Provost of Paris will appoint and dismiss as he will, and they shall swear that they will report truthfully and faithfully the malpractices they find in the guild, and what is reported on oath by all four or by three of them will be believed.

This Tuesday, on the Feast of St Barnabas [11th June], in the year 1303 were elected by the corporation of the guild Jehan de Largi, Jehan d'Argenteil and Ysabel, wife of Guillaume Lebreton.'

The list of some two hundred names of practising craftsmen attached to the original statutes reveals for the first time the extent of male involvement in a craft seen, in more recent times at least, as an exclusively female preserve. Paris, like London, probably had family dynasties of craftsmen, running their own workshops and passing their skills on to the next generation in the family, as well as taking apprentices. The size of these workshops is not known but must surely have varied somewhat. Some will have had fully trained embroiderers (*valets*/journeymen) as well as apprentices at various stages of training, plus the ability to take on additional help for an ambitious project. Others may have been simply a husband-and-wife team, plus, perhaps, an apprentice. Similar statutes issued in 1316 reveal the same embroiderers as in the 1303 statutes, with many husband-and-wife teams such as Jehan d'Argenteil and his wife, Jacques le Broudeur and his wife, Jehan le Fournier and his wife, Nicolas de Losanne and his wife. We know nothing of the kind of work any of these people carried out, but the name of Estienne Chevalier has become familiar through

entries in the French royal accounts. For example, in 1328 he is recorded as having purchased a quantity of household furnishings following the death of the widowed Clemence of Hungary, Queen of France. His purchases included numbers of room- and bed-hangings in blue, black or tan silk or white hemp (some with related tapestries), cushion covers with fleurs-de-lis, curtains of red and white silk, and a silk bed-cover sprinkled with dolphins and with a border incorporating the arms of Hungary. Together with his female business associate, 'Johanne' la Courtière, Chevalier spent the considerable sum of £420 (this amount based on money values in Paris) and assuming there was only one Chevalier, this transaction reveals a new aspect of the business life of professional embroiderers: recycling the luxuries of the rich. In 1324–8 he is recorded supplying similarly ornate embroidery to Mahaut, Countess of Artois and Burgundy.

The regulations contained in the 1292–1303 Paris embroiderers' statutes reflect many attitudes to working practices which were commonly held in the whole craft community at the time. For example, apprenticeship was seen as a fundamental process of training, the only acceptable route into a craft, and was rigidly enforced. The length of the apprenticeship varied according to the demands and complexity of each craft. A period of eight years was laid down for embroidery apprentices in these statutes, one of the longer apprenticeships, and this no doubt took into account the broad range of techniques to be mastered; similar periods of apprenticeship were required for weavers and tapestry-weavers, four to seven years and eight to ten years respectively.

The statutes also carefully protected apprentices from abuse or neglect by their masters or mistresses. City records show that this was a necessary precaution, apprentices sometimes finding they had been taken on by someone unskilled in the craft or who mistreated them. In Paris concern for the quality of work produced by their colleagues caused the leading craftsmen to insist that all masters and mistresses of workshops had to be established in their craft: that is, their work must have been judged and accepted by the leading masters of the craft, and

they must themselves have served an apprenticeship. Having too many apprentices attached to a master or mistress at any one time was seen as detrimental, as it would limit the amount of time and attention given to each apprentice and affect the quality of the work produced.

Once the apprentice years were completed satisfactorily an embroiderer could continue to work for his or her master or mistress as a skilled *valet*/journeyman, having the opportunity one year and one day later to become a master or mistress in his or her own right. Setting up on one's own would be a costly business involving the hire of premises, provision of lodging and clothing for apprentices, and the initial expense of materials; before remuneration could be expected, there might also be the cost of labour to be borne. Thus there was much to recommend the traditional practice of family dynasties pursuing the same craft. Acquisition of the rudiments of the craft in childhood, picked up informally by imitation, led quite naturally to greater technical skills in adulthood, whilst a continuous occupation of premises lessened the overheads; an established reputation and clientele already existed, and a larger workforce could be employed. In some crafts apprentices could be taken alongside members of the family for training.

The working day usually began shortly after sunrise and ended within daylight. In winter, night was reckoned in cities to commence at vespers (6.00 p.m.) changing in summer (after Lent) to compline (9.00 pm). Craftsmen naturally altered these times to suit their own requirements, and the banning of night working was a common practice in crafts where especially fine workmanship was paramount: embroidery, tapestry-weaving, working in linen, and the making of laces of linen or silk thread, for example. Familiarity with surviving specimens demonstrates just how essential good daylight must have been to achieve the fine and regular embroidery seen on many medieval embroideries, and it is evident from the embroiderers' statutes that even the use of candles to supplement daylight on dark winter days was frowned upon. The ban on night working could be a problem in crafts where delays to impatient customers might have serious repercussions, and seems to have been something of a hinderance to the embroiderers. In their next set of regulations, approved in 1316 by the Provost of Paris, the masters of the craft demanded the right to raise the prohibition on night working — but solely when there was great urgency to complete work and on the assumption, they ingenuously insisted, that the work was well done. Leading embroiderers in the great medieval cities of Europe, especially Paris and London, worked for kings, nobles and prelates who could be extremely intolerant of delays and it was essential that some sensible compromise be established. The working day was often long, but the medieval workman was compensated by many religious holidays, whilst the eve of a holiday was also a shorter working day. Incidentally, the demands of rich and noble patrons produced further problems for master embroiderers, it seems, for they, or perhaps merchants, lured skilled workers away from the established workshops to work in their own homes. Understandably this practice aggravated the embroidery masters who found their commitments disrupted and delayed.

With the concern for high standards that has already been noted, embroiderers paid particular attention to the quality of the gold thread which played such an important part in medieval embroideries. The making of this thread was in itself a skilled occupation, attracting a higher salary than embroiderers received. It was made by hand, by spinning narrow strips of gold or silver-gilt around a core of silk threads. Considerable effort was then expended upon couching the gold thread so that it enriched the surface of the embroidery, catching the light and creating decorative surfaces. The use of poor quality thread by embroiderers would certainly diminish the effect of their work, and could prove disastrous if the thread tarnished rapidly. No patron of work of this kind would tolerate such deterioration. Cutting costs to achieve a greater profit margin has always been a temptation, but in the luxury crafts of the large medieval cities, as hard experience had no doubt shown, it could draw the whole craft community into disrepute.

The regulations state firmly that the violation of the Paris craftsmen's rules was punished rigorously, and a sharp eye was apparently kept upon standards and malpractices by the *jurés*, overseers or inspectors drawn from the craft itself. Fines seem to have been the usual punishment for malpractices or violations of the regulations, half being paid to the king and the other half to *jurés* as part-salary 'for their trouble'. Occasionally the burning of poor or incorrectly made goods is mentioned, but there does not seen to be a case recorded which involved embroidery.

By the fifteenth century the Paris regulations refer to embroiderers in the male case only, although it is certain that women were still as active in the craft as formerly. Men, however, were dominant in the organisation of almost every city trade and industry and therefore headed the guilds too. The 1469 regulations reveal the embroiderers' confraternity gathering at the church of Sainte-Opportune in Paris for mass each Sunday and demanding regular contributions from masters and apprentices to support it.

If the London embroiderers had such formally agreed regulations before the fifteenth century they failed to find their way into any surviving contemporary documents. However, many individuals are known, some of whom were clearly leading masters of their day. Robert Ascombe, for example, represented the Brouderers with Nicholas Halley in 1376 on the Common Council of London, and also worked for Richard II in 1394–8. In 1431 'good men of the Mistery of *Brouderers*' presented regulations before the Mayor and Alderman for approval; these chiefly related to the election and duties of the masters. Elected as master that year was John Mounselle, presumably the John Mounshill who, in 1441, was embroiderer to Henry IV. In 1439, however, the Mayor was asked to allow the Warden to continue in office beyond the normally permitted period 'owing to the paucity of good men in the said Mistry', and in 1447 the then Warden John Sewale was involved in a complicated dispute with the whole membership of the guild.

The most interesting and revealing document

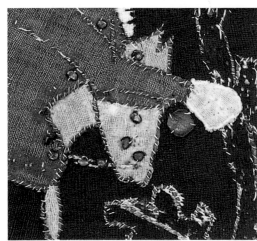

11 *Above* Wall hanging of dark blue cloth with applied figures in coloured cloths and couched gilt leather strip, made in north Germany in the later years of the fourteenth century. Twenty-two scenes from the Tristan legend now survive on this large incomplete hanging. *Right* A detail of St George from the central scene in the bottom row.

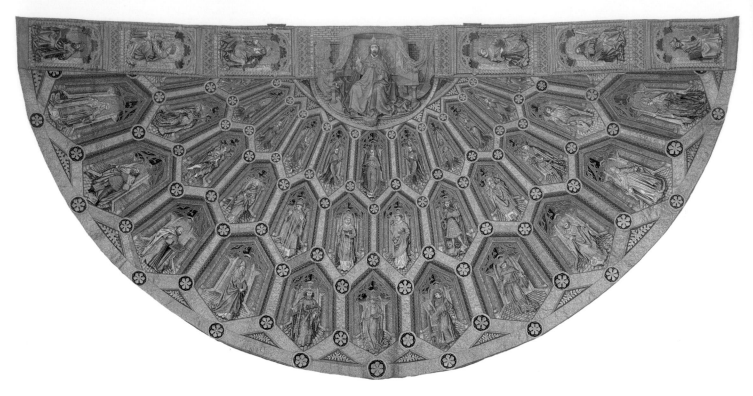

12 Mantle of Christ, from the vestments of the Order of the Golden Fleece. The hood depicts Christ as Ruler of the World; below are angels and cherubims, martyrs and holy princes, bishops and doctors. Mid fifteenth century.

of the London embroiderers was set before the Mayor and Aldermen in 1495 and reveals a link with the Mercers. Much of what they asked had been covered previously in the Paris regulations and was generally understood as common practice in London, but owing to 'certain inconveniences' that had arisen in the craft their petition had clearly become necessary. These 'inconveniences' included the employment of foreign (non-London) embroiderers, faulty work, the use of poor quality threads of silk and gold, incorrect measurements for ecclesiastical vestments, and the use of poorer quality gold thread on velvet, satin or damask. In the latter case it was obviously understood that only best quality thread was appropriate and the embroiderers asked that 'all suche werk to be putt

to fyre and brent or elles to be yeven to poure Churches or Chapelles after your discrecion.' 'Also to ordeigne enacte and establisshe that all Copes vestmentes and tunecles made within this Citee kepe their fulle Shappe in leynth and brede after a lawfull assise of old accustumed upon peyne of xxs. (20s.) for every Cope Vestment and tunecle made to the Contrary' – one half thereof to be to the use of the Chamber, and the other half to go equally to the boxes of the Crafts of Mercers and 'Bouderers'.'

The regulations go on to stipulate that in length a cope should be $1\frac{3}{4}$ yards (1.6 m); a chasuble $1\frac{1}{2}$ yards (1.4 m) and $1\frac{1}{4}$ yards (1.15 m) wide; and a tunicle $1\frac{1}{4}$ yards both in length and width.

Their petition was granted.

3 THE DESIGNERS

In the twentieth century we have become accustomed to designers being household names, celebrities who influence the lives of thousands, sometimes millions, of people. Conceivers of style, they are now mostly separated from the process of manufacture which in turn aims its products at a mass market. In the past this was not the case. Some craftsmen were both designer and maker of their product, although no doubt several copies of a successful 'design' were made in the larger workshops. In the Middle Ages these craftsmen were generally anonymous beyond their local circle, though a few individuals might gain a wider reputation. Whilst some embroiderers may have drawn up their own designs, all would have endeavoured to obtain the services of the most skilled artist available to them. In the tenth century, for example, an Anglo-Saxon noble woman is said

to have sent to St Dunstan (c.909–88) 'and privately entreated him to visit her, that he personally might design for her divers patterns for a stole for divine worship, which she would then execute in varied embroidery of gold and gems.' St Dunstan seems to have been a many-sided man. The present coronation rite of the English sovereign derives from that compiled and used by him for the consecration of Edgar as King of all England at Bath in 973. He was credited with dexterity as a metalworker and bell-founder; he also played the harp, loved the music of the human voice, and was apparently a skilful scribe and draughtsman. It is quite conceivable, therefore, that he turned his artistic skills to embroidery design.

Professional embroiderers certainly used artists to help create the ambitiously ornamented vestments with which we are familiar in

13 Mantle of St Stephen. Worked in couched gold thread on dark blue silk twill, the design shows Christ Victorious and Christ in Majesty, surrounded by prophets, apostles and martyrs, and medallions with portraits of King Stephen and Queen Gisela of Hungary, who commissioned this chasuble and gave it to the church of Szekesfehérvar in 1031. It was subsequently altered and used as the coronation mantle of the Hungarian kings.

14 Italian altar frontal of linen embroidered in silks and gold thread with scenes from the life of the Virgin.

15 Detail of the Coronation of the Virgin, as in fig. 14. Underneath the scene is the inscription *Jacopo Cambi 1336*, presumably the donor of the embroidery. The altar frontal is related in style to works by Bernardo Daddi and his school.

museums today, together with the bed- and wall-hangings which were all the main products of their workrooms. Coupled with the embroiderers' skills, it is the imagination and ingenuity of these artists that we recognise and admire today, but, like the embroiderers, they remain almost completely anonymous.

The involvement of professional artists in the design of embroideries and textiles in medieval Italy is more generously documented. Here, employed by wealthy and enlightened patrons from the Church, the nobility and the merchant classes, artists achieved great individual recognition and fame in their own lifetime. In medieval Italy artists were regarded as all-round craftsmen who could, and would, turn their hand to any work offered to them. It is not surprising, therefore, that a wealthy patron commissioning an expensive altar-frontal like this might turn to 14, 15 an established artist who may already have painted frescoes or panels for him, or may even have designed other embroideries. A similar example is the altar curtain now in Manresa Cathedral in Spain. It was presented to the Cathedral between 1322–57 by Raimondo de Area of Catalonia, but was worked in Florence by an embroiderer called Geri di Lapo – *Geri Lapi rachamatore me fecit in Florentia* – who, by inscribing his embroidery, ensured that his particular achievement should be known to posterity.

It has been suggested that a similar relationship existed in England between the manuscript illuminators and *opus anglicanum*, but this will almost certainly always remain a matter for speculation since so little can be known about the producers of either. Whether the relationship between the illuminators and the embroiderers was direct, the former actually drawing the designs for the latter to work, or indirect, is unclear. What is certain is that the designs for the embroideries reflect a great deal of the drawing style, arrangement and iconography found in contemporary manuscript illuminations. The striking concepts to be found on contents page, 9 such pieces as the great copes and chasubles 10, 16, 6, indicate a mastery of spatial harmony and imagination beyond the common experience. If

16 The Syon Cope (worked 1300–20) derives its name from the Bridgettine convent of Syon, Middlesex, founded by Henry v in 1414–15. It has survived because it was taken by the nuns into exile in the mid sixteenth century and did not return to England until the early nineteenth century. Both the cope and the heraldic orphreys are of linen worked in silk, silver and silver-gilt thread, the former in split stitch, laid and couched work, the latter in underside couching, cross and plait stitch.

the theory of manuscript illuminators as embroidery designers is rejected, then we need to examine the remaining artistic community of London which was, it seems, quite sizeable but which has so far not received a great deal of attention from art historians. Professional artists were employed to ornament walls and woodwork in numerous building projects for the king and the Church. There are also references to them working upon many other artefacts such as pulpits, tombs, chairs (witness the English coronation throne of 1300 at Westminster Abbey), cradles, chests, saddles and carriages. Professional artists were an integral part of the community in a large medieval city like London, selling their skills to whomsoever might seek to employ them, and they may well have designed embroideries for the major producers of *opus anglicanum*, either the master embroiderers or merchants, or rich patrons.

Frustrating though this uncertainty is, we do know a certain amount about the involvement

of artist/designers in the production of decorated clothing, horse-coverings and bed- and wall-hangings in the royal embroidery workshops in London in the 1330s, the end of the great flowering of *opus anglicanum*. Although it is possible that the practices in the royal workshops reflect something of the *opus anglicanum* workshops it must be stressed that radical differences existed between the two. For example, time was always of the essence in the royal household; because of this many shortcuts and quick decorative methods had to be employed, as well as far larger workforces. The artist, therefore, was much in evidence in the workshops as an integral part of the production team, not only drawing up the embroidery designs and supervising the progress and assembling of the work, but also painting heraldic designs on banners, horse-trappings or theatrical costumes, or indeed any other artefact he was instructed to make and ornament. Although time was also a consideration in the creation of fine ecclesiastical embroideries, rapid completion was not so crucial. After all, it was the finely worked labour-consumptive product which was so desired by patrons and shortcuts simply devalued the end product; the development of the latter, indeed, was soon to lead to the decline of *opus anglicanum*. It seems likely, then, that once the artist/designer had drawn up the design for the ecclesiastical embroideries his continued presence was not so necessary.

In the early fourteenth century embroidery at court was almost exclusively the concern of the royal armourer (see chapter 4). Our information about their workshops comes from the now fragmentary accounts presented by the armourers to the accounting clerks of the relevant officers of the royal household. Amongst the expenses listed are numerous references to artists, the most highly paid group within the

workforce and present in some numbers. For the greater part of their time these artists painted heraldic flags and horse-coverings for the king's wars or jousts, or stamped the same sort of decoration in gold or silver on fine silk, again for flags or horse-coverings, but also for bed- and wall-hangings, decorative drapes produced speedily upon demand and with the king's preferred symbols or decorative motifs. Specially commissioned patterned silks were beginning to be produced on the looms of Italy and Spain but, quite apart from their great expense, they must have taken a long time to be produced — too long for an impatient monarch. Stencilling heraldic or animal or foliage designs on silk was achieved much more quickly and at far less expense, factors which no doubt pleased and satisfied the royal patron. The pressing need for an item, usually commissioned for a specific

17 Sir Geoffrey Luttrell with his wife and daughter-in-law. This well-known illumination from the Luttrell Psalter of 1335–40 shows a horse-covering and other knightly accessories of precisely the kind created for the king at this time.

occasion and purpose, made these artists a vital part of their workforce.

They can be found as well drawing quite small motifs for decorating royal clothing: golden squirrels, roses, trees, leopards, silver clouds, eagles, or, that royal symbol particularly associated with Edward III, the garter inscribed with the motto *Honỷ soỷt qe mal ỷ pense* which came to be used in large quantities on royal ceremonial robes in the fourteenth century.

Often several artists worked together and the accounts give the impression that they supervised the embroiderers, tailors and seamstresses brought together to work on a specific project. In 1330, for example, when three counterpanes were embroidered for the elaborate churching ceremonials following the birth of the Black Prince to Edward III and his consort Philippa of Hainault, the Wardrobe accounts show two artist/designers, John de Kerdyff and John de Chidelee, heading the team of 114 during a period of just over three months. John de Kerdyff seems to have been in charge of the work on the counterpanes, being paid 8¼d. per day for the 72 days he spent on the project, whilst his colleague John de Chidelee was paid 6¼d. per day for the 78 days he was involved. The accounts call both men *protrattor*, which we translate as artist or designer. Of the designs worked on the counterpanes all that we know is that they were various 'beasts, babewyns [monkeys or fantastic animals] and knots'.

Whether the armourers worked for clients other than the king is not known. Nor is it certain on what basis the artist/designers were employed by them: if not permanently, then probably contracted in on a daily or weekly basis according to the work available. They came from the London community of painters, some from the known family dynasties of London painters; one or two women from the same families were also employed as painters and gold burnishers in the same royal workshops, but this was unusual. Did some of these artists find themselves drawing up designs for the ecclesiastical embroiderers in London? Regrettably there seems no way of ever discovering this, but their proven involvement with embroidery makes them strong contenders for the honour.

The work of some of the 'designers' of embroideries can be seen on specimens where the stitching has worn away or the dyes have rotted the embroidery silks themselves. These reveal how careful was the preparatory design drawn up by the artist, providing the embroiderers with detailed guidance. The latter, of course, still had to interpret the intentions and style of the artist, and this they will have learned to do during the years of their apprenticeship. Even the details of the patterned grounds of couched gold thread were drawn in for the embroiderers, though worn embroideries reveal that on occasion these were ignored. An interesting, possibly unique, example of linen prepared with drawings of apostles under arches, together with half-length figures of the Virgin, Christ and St John for embroidered vestment orphreys was found in the tomb of San Paranzio. Embroidery of a very crude quality has been worked on part of it, but this in no way does justice to the quality of the original artist's design drawn up in ink.

Some half-century or so later, in the early fifteenth century, the Florentine painter Cennino Cennini composed his manual *Il Libro dell'Arte* 'for the use and good profit of everyone who wants to enter this profession'. It is known in three manuscripts, and the techniques it describes were essentially those in use earlier in the fourteenth century. Covering a wide range of subject-matter, including the problems of applying paint and gold leaf to cloth for banners and hangings, techniques already noted in the London royal workshops, Cennini includes instructions for artists approached by embroiderers for designs:

Again, you sometimes have to supply embroiderers with designs of various sorts. And, for this, get these masters to put cloth or fine silk on stretchers for you, good and taut. And if it is white cloth, take your regular charcoals, and draw whatever you please. Then take your pen and your pure ink, and reinforce it, just as you do on panel with a brush. Then sweep off your charcoal. Then take a sponge, well washed and squeezed out in water. Then rub the cloth with it, on the reverse, where it has not been drawn on; and go on working the sponge until the cloth is damp as far as the figure extends. Then take a small, rather blunt, minever [squirrel] brush; dip it in the ink; and after squeezing it out well you begin to shade with it in the darkest places, coming back and softening gradually. You will find that there will not be any cloth so coarse but that, by this method, you will get your shadows so soft that it will seem to you miraculous. And if the cloth gets dry before you have finished shading, go back with the sponge and wet it again as usual. And let this suffice you for work on cloth.

Stretching materials before they were embroidered was already a well-established practice which Cennini, in an earlier section of his manuscript, advises artists to adopt before painting on cloth. The London designers for embroiderers probably followed a similar procedure, and indeed fine ink lines appear in worn embroidery on many English examples. They are also clearly to be seen by the naked eye on the thirteenth-century gloves of the Holy Roman Empire in Vienna.

Velvet, that most costly silk fabric, offered new problems to artists and embroiderers when it began to be available more generally in the later thirteenth century. It offered a brilliant and rich background for embroidery and was much favoured by patrons wishing to demonstrate their wealth and status. Using the velvet to form the background saved the embroiderers much

labour, but the pile of the velvet made embroidery difficult. 'If you have to work on velvets, or to design for embroiderers,' Cennini advises his readers, 'draw your works with a pen, with either ink or tempered white lead. . . . But it will be less trouble for you to work each thing out on white silk, cutting out the figures or whatever else you do, and have the embroiderers fasten them on your velvet.' Examination of surviving medieval embroideries on velvet reveals that this procedure was indeed followed, though sometimes the embroidery seems to have been worked directly through the fine silk motif and the velvet beneath it. [18]

An English artist's sketch-book of the late fourteenth century at Magdalene College, Cambridge, includes human figures, animals, birds, grotesques, architectural details, and ornament, some of which are reminiscent of fourteenth-century embroideries. These might have been used by a designer working for embroidery workshops, though this can hardly have been the main purpose of the book. It demonstrates the way in which painting and embroidery design interlink. Carefully observed birds, for example, of the type recorded in this sketch-book appear both in the margins of earlier fourteenth-century manuscripts and in the embroideries of the time, whilst the figures are reminiscent of the small figures inhabiting the background foliage of the heraldic fragment of the 1330s associated with Edward III and the London embroidery workshops. [19, 23] [22] [20]

In the fifteenth century artists of standing are more frequently associated with embroidery and the Italian artist and writer Vasari records a number of them. The most famous example is Antonio Pollaiuolo, who designed a set of vestments in 1466 for the Cathedral of S. Maria de Fiore in Florence, so effectively carried out in *or nué*. Already in Flanders the same technique had been worked to stunning effect on the vestments of the Order of the Golden Fleece. It is believed likely that Duke Philip the Good of Burgundy (1419–67) commissioned these vestments for his own chapel prior to the foundation of the Order of the Golden Fleece in 1429, subsequently presenting the vestments to the Order. Nothing is known of the place of origin [21] [12, 48, 4 back cov]

18 Detail of fig. 10, showing the foot of one of the kings in the Adoration scene. The rotting of black silk embroidery stitches has revealed the fine woven silk motif prepared by the draughtsman/ designer of the chasuble, as guidance to the embroiderer.

or of the designers, but artists of the highest calibre undoubtedly contributed, the altar-frontal being associated with the circle of the Master of Flémalle, whilst the cope and dalmatics are in a later style, in the neighbourhood of Rogier van der Weyden. The quality of the embroidery is also of the highest standard,

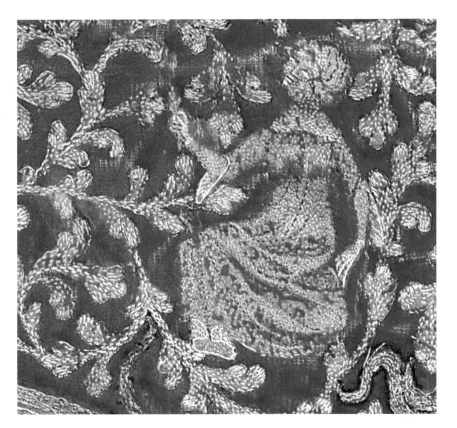

19 *Above* A female figure from the Pepysian sketchbook which is of the sort to have been the inspiration for fig. 20.

20 *Above right* Detail of female figure from the ground decoration of one side of an heraldic embroidery (see fig. 25 for the other piece) similar to figures in the Pepysian sketchbook.

21 *Right* Portrait by Filippino Lippi (1457–1504) of the artist Antonio Pollaiuolo.

22 *Right* Detail of orphrey embroidery on the Pienza Cope (*see contents page*) showing realistically depicted birds similar to those recorded in fig. 23.

23 *Above* Page of bird drawings from the Pepysian sketchbook by an English artist.

doing full justice to the delicate underpainting revealed in worn areas.

A little later, Pierre de Villant, painter and embroiderer to René d'Anjou, designed a complete chapel for the Cathedral of Angers. These were all of gold embroidery and comprised a chasuble, tunicle, dalmatic and cope; the altar apparel showed the Passion of our Lord. On 4 March 1462 a mass of the Holy Spirit was sung by the Chapter in the presence of the Duke and Duchess of Anjou for the reception of this work of art. It became known as *La Grande Broderie* (many inventories reveal names of this sort given to magnificent embroideries) and survived until the French Revolution, when it was slashed and burned for its gold.

4 PRODUCTION

It is an irony of history that so much fine ecclesiastical embroidery survives with little supporting documentary evidence showing how it was designed and produced, whilst a wealth of documentary evidence for the production of lavishly ornamented royal clothing, in fourteenth-century London and Paris, is still available but is itself supported by virtually no surviving examples. However, this detailed information about the production of embroidery for secular uses provides valuable insight into the practices of medieval workshops and is bound to reflect at least some aspects of the production of fine ecclesiastical embroidery, including *opus anglicanum*. Careful examination of surviving embroideries both reveals and confirms details of manufacture, supporting, or adding to, knowledge drawn from documentary sources.

Although now fragmentary, the financial accounts of the English and French royal households are fruitful sources of information about medieval clothing production; here, we see officials at their work buying or commissioning goods for their extravagant masters. Cloths, silks, linens and furs were purchased in quantity and distributed as required to the royal tailors and armourers. So, too, were ribbons, braids, threads of silk, linen or gold for sewing and embroidery, and a multitude of other workroom necessities, the listing of which for accounting purposes reveals so much to us today.

From the information currently available it seems likely that embroidery was used rarely and sparingly upon secular garments in the earlier Middle Ages, the stunning continental coronation mantles being exceptions which have been especially treasured. Richly woven silks from Spain, Italy, the Near East and, when available, China, satisfied many of the cravings for ornate dress throughout the earlier Middle Ages, just as they continued to do in succeeding centuries. But, as we have seen, embroidery has early origins in Europe and was an integral part of its cultural expression. An embroidery like the Bayeux Tapestry represents another, and

24 Craftsmen at work on embroidered hangings, from a north Italian manuscript of *c.*1400. The illustration comes from a picture book of scenes from the Book of Exodus in which Bezalehel and Oliab are shown making liturgical objects for use in the tabernacle. The large upright frames are unusual, leading many to believe that weaving is being depicted. This is not so, however, as the craftsmen are clearly adding decoration to fabric already stretched within the frames. It has recently been suggested that these tabernacle hangings are of *lacis*, a hand-knotted net ground with decoration added in a needle-weaving technique.

highly impressive, application of the craft for purposes of decoration and status, and a corpus of work now almost wholly lost. The working of such large hangings must also have influenced the size and management of early embroidery workshops, but we know nothing at all of the circumstances under which such pieces were created.

Instructions were brought back to the workshops by the royal armourer, obtained directly from the king, or, in some instances, relayed by a court official. Written instructions or commissions for embroidery rarely survive beyond those confirming the verbal instructions already issued. By the beginning of the fourteenth century royal demand became more extensive and special workshops began to be set up to deal with it. The information provided for accounting purposes by the heads of these workshops includes the types, costs and quantities of materials provided, as well as the amount and cost of labour involved in the making of an individual item. Sometimes the labour costs were broken down, so that we know how many workers were involved, the levels of wages for different skills, and the length of time contributed by individuals. Very occasionally the names of the workers are mentioned too, affording us a detailed insight into the workforce, the range of skills they offered, their salary differentials, and the balance of male and female workers.

For example, in 1330 the three counterpanes embroidered for the churching ceremonials of Queen Philippa required a workforce of 112 people headed by two artist/designers: 70 men earning $4\frac{1}{2}$d. per day, and 42 women earning $3\frac{1}{4}$d. per day, whilst the artist/designers earned $8\frac{1}{4}$d. and $6\frac{1}{4}$d. per day respectively, a total of £60 17s. 6d. It is not known how the work was divided between the team or the sexes, although they would presumably divide into three groups, each working on a single counterpane. Beams, cord, thick thread and hooks were purchased for the work by the Queen's tailor William de London, who also arranged the preparation, by beating and fluffing up, of the cotton wool for the mattresses and one of the counterpanes, and purchased candle-wax for

sealing the raw edges of the silk and cotton. This practice is referred to from time to time in the accounts, and traces of wax have been found sealing the raw edges of silk on embroidered motifs, worked first before being cut out and applied to their final position. Wax was also used to seal the painting on banners and streamers, and on linen to make water-resistant covers for transporting royal clothing, bedding and room-hangings. The task of the royal tailor, it has to be noted, extended beyond supervising the making of clothes, to organising bedding and other private necessities.

At the same time an impressive set of garments was prepared for Queen Philippa. The accounting records for that year reveal that although her tailor William de London himself received the purple velvet for the *robe* (a set of five garments) from the Great Wardrobe officials, he took it, almost certainly cut out by him into garment pieces, to the workshops of John de Cologne, the King's armourer, where it was ornamented with golden squirrels. This seems to have been the first embroidered garment made in London for the young Flemish Queen, and she, her husband and her family were to indulge this extravagant taste in successive decades, loyally served by John de Cologne for much of that time.

The accounts for this year are incomplete and the final total of labour costs of £68 5s. 5d. suggests a workforce similar in size to that already at work on the counterpanes. John de Cologne found it necessary to buy iron hooks and thick cord and thread for this project plus some unidentified items termed *stodeles*, perhaps beams or frames for stretching the work, purchased from a carpenter. Other components purchased for this work included 162 ells of Cologne sindon (probably a fine linen cloth), 14 lb of gold and 16 lb of silk thread (including 4 lb each of white and black thread), a total of £43 1s. 10d., to which must be added William de London's modest labour costs of £2 8s. $2\frac{3}{4}$d. for cutting and putting together the garment pieces. The cost of the velvet itself is not recorded but must have been in the region of £72, plus about £16 for the fur linings. The total expenditure on this one set of garments was therefore about £201 15s. 5¾d., more than many medieval workers might earn in their lifetime.

The requirement for speed engendered by impatient royal requests frequently meant that motifs in contrasting colours (appliqué) were used to create ornament, especially heraldic motifs. A typical example of this was a jousting tunic made for Edward III in 1345–9 when red and blue cloth formed the fields of his quartered arms, and yellow cloth the heraldic symbols of leopards passant guardant and fleurs-de-lis. It was a technique especially appropriate to the huge ornamental tents used by the King and his household to extend their summer living-quarters. Cennino Cennini mentions the use of tailor's chalk for drawing on black or blue cloth, made neatly into little pieces 'just as you do with charcoal; and put them into a goose-feather quill, of whatever size is required. Put a little stick into this quill, and draw lightly. Then fix with tempered white lead.' Practical details of this kind rarely emerge from the royal accounts but one entry in 1330–1 includes the purchase, for 9d., of six skins of parchment for making the pattern (*patron*) of the leopards on a tunic of arms where the leopards were worked in gold thread; in the same account two quires of paper were purchased for 6d. in connection with a

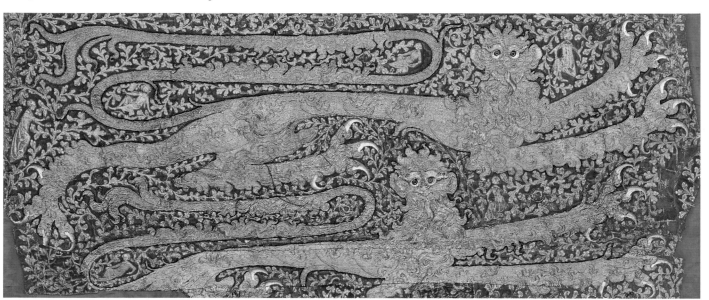

25, 26

26 *Below* Fragment of heraldic embroidery showing the three leopards of England worked in surface-couched gold thread and coloured silks. This is believed to have been a horse-covering made for Edward III in 1330–40 and perhaps presented to a convent during a visit to Coblenz in 1338.

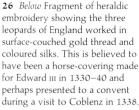

25 *Above* Detail of leopard's head from fig. 26 showing the lively couching technique and glass disc eyes.

heraldic horse-covering stamped with silver and gold leaf.

Another solution to the demands for speed was the use of repetitive motifs, which became an important element in the design of secular, and later ecclesiastical, embroidery. Not only did the process minimise the use of the artist's time, but it also meant that the motifs could be prepared individually by a larger team of embroiderers, and then quickly assembled on a garment or hanging.

The speed at which ornate items had to be created is well demonstrated by an order on 8 September 1352 to the *armeurier au Roy et brodeur* Nicholas Waquier for a horse-covering and room-hanging of velvet ornamented with fleurs-de-lis. The pieces were to be completed by All Saints (1 November), and in that time 8544 embroidered fleurs-de-lis had to be produced and attached to the various items involved. Needless to say we find 'les fleurs de lis broudees jour et nuit en grant haste' and the embroiderers aided in their work by the provision of candles and wine.

The English royal arms (three leopards) did not lend themselves so readily to this sort of approach, but the founding of the Order of the Garter in the 1340s by Edward III provided, in the garters associated with the Order, just such a repetitive motif. John de Cologne was responsible for making the first garters, which presumably were functional, of blue taffeta embroidered in gold and silk with the motto *Honÿ soÿt qe mal ÿ pense*. He created many more garters to ornament flags, bed-hangings, horse-coverings and garments. Quite what form these took at this early date is not altogether clear. Two *jupouns* (tunics for armour) of blue satin and taffeta each seem to have been ornamented with sixty-two garter motifs, each with a silver-gilt buckle and pendant, whilst 168 similar garter motifs were applied to a cloak, supertunic, tunic and hood of blue cloth for the King. In successive years, to celebrate the Feast of St George, patron saint of the Order, similar garter-ornamented garments were produced for the King, his knights, and members of his family, and by the beginning of the reign of his grandson Richard II (1377–99) the King's Em-

broiderer, in this case Hans de Strowesburgh (? John Strousburgh, see page 50), found himself supplying 2000 garter motifs for the twenty-six robes required for the young King and his fellow knights. They seem to have had new robes each year, and so this mass-production process was repeated annually in the workshops of the Embroiderer, a straightforward but, one imagines, rather boring task. These robes seem subsequently to have been turned into church vestments, as many later appear in the inventories of City churches.

27

27 *Opposite* The so-called 'Eagle Dalmatic', part of the insignia of the Holy Roman Empire, first recorded in 1350. Created in Austria in about 1320, it has circular medallions of embroidered eagles with black glass eyes applied to a ground of Chinese purple silk damask of about 1300 or earlier; thirty-nine crowned kings feature on the embroidered orphreys.

28 Badge of the Order of the Dragon, gold thread couched in coloured silks, with a glass bead forming the eye. The Badge was originally worn on a mantle of the Order which was founded by King Sigismund of Hungary (1414–37) to combat the infidel.

Production of these repetitive motifs was aided by tracing the design onto paper, pricking the outline, and then transferring the design on to cloth any number of times by pouncing with powdered chalk, pumice or charcoal. When the paper was lifted, rows of fine dots of powder lay revealed, and these in turn could be fixed with ink or paint; the surplus powder could then be blown away. A woodcut in one of the earliest printed books for embroiderers, Alessandro Paganino's *Libro Primo . . . de rechami* (1527) shows women tracing, pricking and transferring embroidery designs, using natural light and candlelight to aid tracing. Paper production began to increase only during the fourteenth century but by the time Cennino Cennini was writing it was possible, in Italy at least, to obtain very thin white paper, 'Then grease this paper with linseed oil . . . It becomes transparent, and it is good.' Failing this one could employ a much older method using parchment carefully scraped to make it transparent and then similarly treated with linseed oil.

On occasion parchment or paper might form the foundation of an embroidered motif (see page 53), helping to preserve its shape from distortion during the embroidery process and such evidence is found from time to time by conservators.

Of the more practical aspects of the embroiderers' workshops and equipment we gain only fleeting glimpses. Although the accounts presented to the royal households for payment carefully detail all the components used in the making of each item, the materials, linings, paddings, ornaments, threads, ribbons or braids, fastenings and, where appropriate, candles for lighting, together with their cost, there are certain notable exceptions. Needles, pins and shears or scissors might have been expected to appear occasionally as expenses, but they never do and we have to suppose that already, by established tradition, the craftsmen were supplying their own equipment. Many of these artefacts survive in archaeological contexts although never the needles used for fine em-

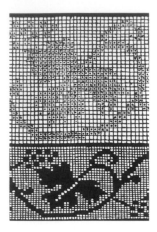

broidery: being so thin, they have long since perished. Pins were much used in the past for holding clothing in place during wear and so are occasionally mentioned in royal trousseaux, and their use in an embroidery workshop seems reasonably assured. If medieval illuminations showing craftsmen at work are to be trusted, even at this early date they kept their threads and equipment tidily in a basket. Sticks had long been used for measuring cloth, and no doubt similar measuring devices were also used in the embroiderers' workshops as well as some early form of tape measure. As far as we know no reels or spools for thread existed, but silk threads have been found wound on sticks.

The use of wooden frames for stretching embroideries may have been going on for several centuries. The cloth was stretched over the frame and tacked into place so that tension and threads were even. The evidence seems to suggest that embroiderers were stretching their ground on the frame in a slightly different manner to that general in more recent times, but this was presumably based upon experience. Illustrations of medieval embroiderers at work

show the ground stretched within a larger frame, pulled taut by a strong thread whipped round the frame at regular intervals. The purchase of strong thread (packthread) or cord for the embroiderers supports this. Frames offered the best conditions for working upon embroideries, large or small, and could be extremely adaptable. Supported by one or two trestles (a support formed by a short beam with diverging legs) they became like a table. Larger frames could also have an edge rested between a table and a trestle, and this practice of working has continued into recent times. Trestle tables themselves are known to have been used in these workshops and could be of any size.

The windows of these craftsmen's workrooms would not usually have been glazed until late in the Middle Ages. Instead they would have wooden shutters, normally on hinges, which were closed at night. However, on occasion these open windows presented problems and entries in the accounts show canvas or linen being placed over them to keep out the wind, rain or even snow. The embroidery was presumably protected from dust or other damage during work but in only one or two specific instances are linen cloths provided 'to protect the work from the embroiderers' own hands'. This would be particularly important, of course, where white or light-coloured grounds were involved, and also in work with gold thread since natural moisture from the hands could act like an acid, tarnishing the thread.

Preparation for the embroideries to leave the workshop was careful, leaving little to chance. Past disasters had obviously shown that all eventualities should be expected and guarded against. The finished items were carefully enveloped in linen and canvas, and sometimes waxed linen covers were used to repel moisture. They were then placed in leather bags or even travelling chests if they were large. Their cross-country journey, which might extend across the sea and continent, was usually in an open cart with a large leather cover. Thus the embroiderers ensured that their patient labours and patron's investment were well and truly protected so that their skills might be fully appreciated wherever they eventually found a home.

29 *Above* Printed embroidery designs showing the pattern indicated by dots and squares. *Above right* Women transferring embroidery designs by pricking and pouncing. See page 64.

5 TECHNIQUES

Embroidery is a term widely used to describe decoration applied to a textile by the use of stitching techniques. The earliest examples in Europe demonstrate that the craft had a long and ancient history, whose origins are not known. In the Middle Ages more archaic forms survived in rural or distant areas, favoured by the less affluent or socially less ambitious, whilst wealthy patronage encouraged the development of more complex and more sophisticated techniques in cities. Some of these embroideries are extremely famous, especially the fine labour-consumptive examples worked for the Church (*opus anglicanum*) or for royal patrons; these have been admired and safeguarded through the centuries and are now mostly owned by the great museums of the world. Beyond these, however, there remains a surprising range of embroidery techniques to be found in medieval Europe, some known only through small frag-

ments, others almost solely from documentation.

APPLIQUÉ

This is a very simple and rapid method of obtaining decorative effect by stitching cloth pieces to a contrasting ground. It was especially effective when using the well-fulled medieval cloths, whose cut edges did not readily fray and could easily be held by hem-stitching. It was less effective on silks or velvets because of the fraying problem; the edges could be protected by couched threads or cords, whilst bees-wax has been found on the raw edges of some medieval pieces. Only a small number of examples of this decorative approach now survive, but documentary sources show that it was extremely widely used, either for quick effect or, in less affluent areas of society, to use up small pieces of cloth and discarded cloth; it

30 Fragment of English heraldic embroidery featuring the arms of William de Fortz, third count of Aumale (*d*.1260) alternating with those of his second wife Isabel (*m*.1248). The original form of the embroidery is not known, but at some later date it was reused as a seal bag.

31 *Above* Seal bag attached to a charter of Edward I dated at Westminster, 26 November 1280, and probably of the same date.

32 *Above right* German fifteenth-century chasuble of dark blue wool with applied ornamentation in linen and coloured cloths depicting the Crucifixion and the instruments of the Passion. The details are in silk thread and there is a parchment strip which was possibly gilded. The drawing of Christ is in brown ink.

was referred to as *opus consutum* and lingers to the present day in folk-embroidery.

31   A seal bag at Westminster Abbey displays a refinement of the appliqué technique, the use of *intarsia* or inlaid motifs: the shield was cut to shape and laid in a mirror image cut in the ground. Having been sewn into place, thread or cord was couched along the join lines, whilst the leopards were applied on top and such details as the leopards' tails, eyes and claws added afterwards using split-stitch. An even more economic and decorative effect was achieved when exactly similar motifs were cut from contrasting pieces of cloth and the motifs exchanged. This of course was inappropriate to heraldic motifs, but is a decorative element found particularly in

35   Scandinavia.

Documentary sources also indicate that decorative wall-hangings were made in this way before tapestry-woven hangings were widely available. A surviving hanging from north Germany, ornamented with scenes from the

11   Tristan legend, shows what attractive possessions these hangings were and how well the technique lent itself to narrative. Sewn around the edges of the motifs are the remains of narrow gilded leather strips imitating couched gold thread, an effect much used on Scandinavian medieval hangings, most of which have designs of roundels containing animals. Indeed it is very likely that many of these hangings employed less worn areas of used clothing; recycling of expensive materials in this way was common practice in the Middle Ages and succeeding centuries.

OUTLINE AND FILLING STITCHES
A line of stitching, made by running, double-running, back- or stem-stitch, is the most obvious way of creating a decorative motif on the surface of a woven ground. Not surprisingly, therefore, these are some of the earliest

stitches to appear on pre-medieval embroideries which survive today. Of these stitches it was stem, or outline, stitch which was to predominate as an outline stitch throughout the Middle Ages. With its overlapping technique it formed a strong outline especially suitable for curves and was one of the most important stitches used on the Bayeux Tapestry, where it was combined with couched infilling to create a large-scale, lively narrative embroidery. It is an easy stitch for novices to master, quickly worked and producing effective results in a short time.

Split- and chain-stitches were also used on the Bayeux Tapestry, both, like stem-stitch, effective outline stitches. Of these, split-stitch is very similar to stem stitch and became one of the preferred stitches of *opus anglicanum*, often worked extremely finely and densely, especially for faces and hands. Here it followed the contours of the features, making the modelling very lifelike, and so fine that the individual lines of stitches merge to form a cohesive mass. Elsewhere, on hair and drapery particularly, the fineness of the lines of stitchery enables shading to be carried out so that at a distance the result very much resembles manuscript illumination. Chain-stitch, a progression of loop stitches, was also used in the same way in medieval em-

broidery, but it is rather less effective as the individual stitches do not merge.

THREAD COUNTING

Embroidery which makes direct use of the warp and weft threads of linen has a long history, longer perhaps than many embroiderers today realise; several such techniques seem to have been especially popular in medieval Germany and Switzerland. Cross-stitch, counted-thread and drawn-thread work feature in many surviving examples in convents, church treasuries and museums. They are also found in the repertoire of other European countries – Italy, Spain and England, for example – but appear not to have come into prominent use in these countries until the end of the Middle Ages.

Cross-stitch and counted-thread embroidery are both quickly mastered. Their repetitious nature meant that they produced effective ornament in a fairly short period of time, covering the ground of the work much more rapidly than the finer, more painstaking, needle-painting techniques. A wide variety of infill patterns could be devised in counted-thread work, the combination of which produced very decorative results, even in monochrome embroidery. Some counted-thread stitches could pull together small groups of threads to produce a decorative net-like effect. Drawn-thread work is rather more demanding, requiring careful preparation through the removal of selected warp and weft threads and the manipulation by stitching methods of the remaining threads into an open patterned web-like ground. By the end of the Middle Ages it was widely popular, with elaborate lace-like effects created by the use of additional threads woven in with a needle.

These whitework embroideries were known in the Middle Ages as *opus teutonicum* and their obvious concentration in Germany has led writers to speculate whether it was a sign of poverty, of the lack of means in north German convents in particular to purchase costly foreign silk threads, that this form of embroidery became so typical of Germany at the time. It was certainly very recognisable and found its way into cathedral treasuries elsewhere. A great many of the pieces seem to have been worked in

34 *Above* One of a pair of seal bags protecting the Great Seals on charters of 8 June 1319. It is worked in cross and split stitch and underside couching, and is probably of the same date. Both seal bags bear the arms of the City of London, a shield with St Paul holding a sword and a book.

35 *Right* Detail from a Swedish fifteenth-century coverlet of applied work in red, blue and white cloth, with couched gilded leather strips.

convents in the area, the designs created for the nuns by wandering craftsmen and painters; indeed, many are still in the convents where they were made. The embroideries were made for the service of the Church, as altar-cloths, chalice-veils and Lenten veils.

One of the earliest surviving examples of cross-stitch is the twelfth-century chasuble from the Benedictine monastery of St Blasien in the Black Forest. Completely worked in long-armed cross-stitch, in coloured silks on a linen ground, it has thirty-eight compartments enclosing scenes from the Old and New Testaments and the saints; in the border are medallions with half-length figures of prophets, evangelists, apostles and princes. The sparing use of gold, sometimes avoided altogether, is typical of early medieval German embroidery and was compensated for by the extremely rich effect of the colourful silks.

Another counted-thread stitch especially popular in continental Europe was brick-stitch, a variant of satin-stitch. Groups of two or three stitches worked side by side over the same number of woven threads were used to fill out areas of colour or to make patterns within areas, helping to build up designs over the whole of a linen ground. It seems to have been particularly popular for cushions worked with repeating motifs within compartments, like the well-preserved cushion from the Treasury of Enger; similar cushions often appear in paintings and as head supports for tomb effigies. It is likely that

36 *Above* Fourteenth-century German altarcloth of linen embroidered in white linen thread (photographed against light to show the design more clearly) from the Convent of Altenberg, on the Lahn.

37 *Below* Linen cushion embroidered in coloured silks in brick stitch, from the Treasury of Enger; fourteenth or fifteenth century, Westphalia.

37

they were fairly common and that this form of embroidery was widespread. Vestments and large hangings worked in brick-stitch seem to have been especially common in Germany. A late fourteenth-century church-hanging, believed to have been worked by nuns and now shown in the treasury of The Cloisters in New York, demonstrates the colourful and decorative effect achieved by this technique. Brick stitch could be used to equal effect in linen thread on linen, often in combination with other counted thread stitches to enhance the decorative effect. An impressive example of this kind of work is a mid fourteenth-century altar-cloth from Hesse, where a great variety of infilling patterns was used to form the figures and foliage making up the design. An inscription recording the names of the embroideresses – Hadewigis, Sophia and Lucardis, abbess and nuns in the Praemonstratensian convent of Altenberg on the Lahn – was worked into the embroidery.

QUILTING

Surviving examples of medieval quilting are exceptionally rare. Unspun wool or cotton sandwiched between two pieces of linen had long

been used in the creation of protective doublets for wear under chain mail or plate armour. Some stitching was used to keep all layers in place, either vertical or diagonal cross-hatching, and this is frequently indicated in tomb effigies and manuscript illuminations. Garments of this kind were the responsibility of the tailors and linen armourers in major western cities like Paris and London from the thirteenth century at least.

The practice possibly originated in the Near East or India but it is not known when more decorative and elaborate quilting came into use in Europe. The mastery of the technique evident in the large Tristan quilt worked in Sicily at the end of the fourteenth century suggests several centuries of evolution.

Only small amounts of cotton wool were used in the Tristan quilt, in the 'stuffed quilting' technique where the cotton wool was introduced at the back of the work after the decorative stitching had been carried out. The ground of the work between the motifs was worked with close rows of running stitches in white linen thread, whilst the outlines of the figures, ships and buildings were worked in back-stitch in a brownish thread.

38 *Above left* Detail from a late fourteenth-century German linen altar hanging worked with biblical scenes in coloured silks in brick stitch, and a border with saints, and the arms of the Landgrave of Hesse and the House of Lichtfuss.

39 Detail from the Guicciardini quilt showing Tristan and the Morold fighting on the isle of Santa Vintura.

40 One half of the Guicciardini quilt, believed to be Sicilian work of about 1400; the second part is in the Museo Nazionale, Florence. The whole ground of this unique quilt shows scenes from the Tristan legend, of the oppression of Cornwall by King Languis of Ireland and his champion the Morold. This fragment measures 3.1 m by 2.69 m (10′2″ by 8′10″).

39

A large fragment of a German coverlet of the 42 fifteenth century is made of a much coarser linen worked firmly in back-stitch with stylised animal motifs within octagonal compartments formed by corded quilting, a method whereby a cord of plied cotton thread was introduced after the parallel lines of back-stitches had been worked. This is a very early example of the technique and an equally interesting example of the combination of stuffed and corded quilting.

COUCHING

In couched work threads are laid in parallel lines on the upper surface of the ground and then held in place by stitching so that solid blocks of colour are formed. It was a widely used technique in the Middle Ages, easy to master, and sometimes a linen ground could be completely covered in this way, using wool, silk or gold thread. Thus the need for expensive imported silk grounds was eliminated, an important consideration in less affluent areas of Europe. Decorative effects, particularly narrative designs or symbolic motifs, could be achieved relatively rapidly and in conjunction with other ground-covering embroidery stitches. Much used for wool embroidery in Germany, to judge from the quantity of surviving examples, this embroidery technique helped to economise on the very expensive hand-made gold thread which was quickly damaged when used for other embroidery stitches.

WOOL AND SILK
In that most famous medieval embroidery, the Bayeux Tapestry, couched woollen threads are used to great effect to give solid form to the main elements of the narrative – the men, their horses and their ships – so that they stand out boldly from the linen ground. Already in the late eleventh century the couching technique was of some considerable age: it appears, for example, on a fragment of wool of the first century BC, excavated in Northern Mongolia but believed to have originated in Iran.

The Bayeux Tapestry bears witness to a high 60 level of competence and interpretative skill in the use of this technique, and almost certainly represents a widely deployed corpus of decor-

41 A scene from the Guicciardini quilt showing 'How King Languis sent to Cornwall for the tribute'; the two ambassadors sit in the poop with a banner above them bearing three fleurs-de-lis.

42 Detail from a large German coverlet with corded border and stuffed quilted bird motif.

43 *Top left* The Genesis Hanging, a large eleventh-century Spanish hanging or red woollen twill worked in coloured wools in a stem, chain, satin and a form of couching stitch. In the centre is Christ as Ruler of the World, surrounded by scenes from the story of the Creation. The border shows a figure of the year (*Annus*) between squares showing the Four Seasons, Samson and a man with a sheep. In the two top corners are the Rivers of Paradise; in the side borders, representations of the Months, together with circles showing *Dies Solis* and *Dies Lunae*; at the bottom, the Discovery of the Cross. Nothing is known of the history of the hanging, but the inscription indicates that it was made in the border country of Spain.

44 *Top right* Detail of *Dies Solus* from the Genesis Hanging.

45 *Above* The Malterer Hanging, a German embroidery of about 1310–20 in coloured wools in convent and stem stitch on a linen ground. It illustrates the evil consequences of earthly love: Aristotle and Delilah, Aristotle and Phyllis, Virgil and the daughter of the Emperor Augustus, Iwein and Laudine. The last scene is a symbol of Christian love and chastity: the Virgin with a Unicorn. At both ends are the arms of the Malterer family, who gave the hanging to the Convent of St Catherine at Freiburg i. Breisgau, where Anna Malterer was a nun.

ative hangings now completely lost. A large hanging from Spain, of a slightly later date, has the whole woollen ground obscured by woollen threads couched to form a bold design. This latter technique is particularly characteristic of fourteenth- and fifteenth-century secular German hangings, and of linen embroideries worked chiefly in Switzerland and on the upper Rhine from the fifteenth to seventeenth centuries.

Two methods of couching the threads were employed on these woollen hangings. The first consisted of a ground of laid threads with, at right angles and across them, widely spaced couched threads, as on the Bayeux Tapestry; this method continued in Scandinavian and Icelandic embroideries for several centuries. Alternatively the laid thread could be couched

46 Detail of Iwein and Laudine from the Malterer Hanging (see fig. 45).

as work progressed across the ground, row by row; in wool this approach led to a stitch variously known as convent or Bokhara stitch which was easy to work and quickly produced a solid ground, requiring a single thread only.

Areas of laid silk threads underneath a decorative network of couched silk or gold threads can occasionally be found representing seat-coverings or cushions, but otherwise larger areas of silk were worked in split- or chain-stitch because of the need to sculpt facial features or drapery folds. Silk thread was too fine and vulnerable to be exposed to the rapid damage inevitable if it had been laid and couched in large areas.

GOLD
Both the above methods of couching were also used for couching gold threads. This thread was extremely expensive and the most economical

47 Purse (*aumonière*) depicting lovers, worked in Paris in about 1340. Linen embroidered in silk in split, chain, stem and knot stitches, the background of gold threads couched with red silk.

48 Detail from the Mantle of the Virgin, one of the vestments of the Order of the Golden Fleece. Painters of the circles of the Master of Flémalle and Rogier van der Weyden have been suggested as designers. Mid fifteenth century. (See also back cover.)

use of it was to take the thread backwards and forwards across the surface of the ground, holding it in place by fine silk stitches. In time these holding stitches came to form a subtle decorative element on the couched threads themselves, the silk stitches placed with great precision to form zigzags, diaper grounds or other decorative motifs, further enhanced by the use of coloured threads, usually of red or blue silk. Thick cotton threads could be used as padding underneath the gold couching, giving a third dimension to the couched area; this work demanded yet greater skills and precision from

the embroiderers if the desired effect was to be achieved, for the padding easily distorted the regular lines of couched threads.

In the fifteenth century coloured couching threads were used even more strikingly in the technique known as *or nué* (shaded gold). Here the couching stitches were used to create solid blocks of colour over the gold thread, and became a new form of needle-painting, developed to an impressive level of sophistication by embroiderers in Italy and Flanders in particular. Whole scenes could be created, subtle shading effects being achieved by careful gradations of

49 St Louis, from the lower register of the Mantle of Christ (fig. 12).

50 *Below* Medallion embroidered in couched gold and silver thread, from a set of twenty-four originally from a bishop's cope of crimson silk. The scene of the Presentation of Christ in the Temple is surrounded by the inscription *He who rules the heavenly temple visits the earthly [temple]*. The embroidery is attributed to a north French atelier of the end of the twelfth century.

coloured silks, coupled with variable spacing of the stitches; small gaps, either intentional or accidental, allowed glints from the gold thread beneath and much enhanced the moulding of form and impression of richness.

The Netherlandish mass vestments of the Order of the Golden Fleece, founded in 1429 by Duke Philip the Good of Burgundy, are amongst the most outstanding examples of *or nué* now in existence. Worn areas reveal the delicate under-painting which was to guide the hands of the embroiderers who faithfully and skilfully trans-lated the artist's intentions, their precise and regular stitching naturally enhancing the fin-ished effect; photographs barely do justice to these outstanding examples of needle-painting.

12, 48, back cover

UNDERSIDE COUCHING

50

An interesting variant of couching which de-manded the very greatest skills, this technique is much less familiar to twentieth-century em-broiderers. Although used extensively through-out the Middle Ages its use declined in the fifteenth century and it was superseded by the simpler surface couching. In underside couching the thread, usually gold but occasionally silver or silk, was laid on the upper surface of the ground and was held in place by a loop of linen thread brought from the back of the work. As it returned to the back the linen thread took with it a tiny loop of gold thread, thus entirely concealing itself and firmly anchoring the laid thread. This method of couching produced an embroidered surface which had a far greater degree of flexibility than was otherwise poss-ible, and its method of drawing the gold thread into the body of the ground offered the thread greater protection from wear. Patterned grounds were often created on the upper surface by varying the placing of the stitches or by confining the laid threads to separate areas of the ground, and were very skilled sophistica-tions. Most medieval embroideries do seem to have been worked whilst stretched on em-broidery frames, but this particular technique could be worked only under tension thus, as it appears to have been in use quite early in medi-eval embroidery, emphasising the sophisticated nature of the later Anglo-Saxon embroideries.

ENRICHMENT OF EMBROIDERY

Elaborate medieval embroideries were often further enriched by the addition of pearls and 51 other precious and semi-precious stones, gold or silver ornaments, enamelled plaques or, very occasionally at this period, glass beads or discs, whilst some are almost exclusively composed of these ornaments and might not properly be considered as embroideries. These powerful symbols of status and wealth were at least as widely seen in the Church as in royal or aristocratic courts: many of these rich creations were the gift of wealthy patrons seeking influence or favours. However, it would eventually be this very enrichment which ensured the destruction of these pieces, for once the gold, jewels and pearls were removed, the ground would quickly be recycled. So much of this work has disappeared that it can now be difficult to envisage the extravagance involved, though the imagination is aided by fifteenth-century paintings which, with their naturalistic and precise approach, frequently portray these jewel-enriched garments. Coupled with the boldly designed and coloured Italian silks and velvets the effect must indeed have been sumptuous and impressive.

Pearls were very popular in the Middle Ages, especially tiny seed pearls, which were much used in place of jewels in crowns, or to form haloes, birds, masks, or other decorative motifs. English royal accounts of the fourteenth century reveal that these pearls cost between £1 and £2 per ounce. Together with a range of other, larger pearls, some coloured, originating from the East or from Scotland, they were frequently employed upon festal or jousting garments at the French and English courts and often massed together to form decorative motifs. In 1345–9, for example, Edward III's armourer John de

51 Cuff detail of the deep purple silk dalmatic of 1130–40 from the insignia of the Holy Roman Empire. It is a product of the royal workshops of Roger II in Palermo. Minute golden tubes fill the pearl motifs whilst the sumptuous effect is increased by the use of large coloured enamel motifs.

52 John the Fearless, Duke of Burgundy, being presented with a copy of *Hayton's Travels*, from a French manuscript of 1410. The Duke is dressed extravagantly in richly-embroidered fur-lined robes.

Cologne made five hoods of white cloth for the King and his friends, each worked with blue dancing men and fastening at the front with buttons of large pearls. They required 2350 large pearls, together with velvet, silk and gold thread. These richly embroidered hoods were fashionable at the time and there are many entries listing the expensive requirements for them.

The mitre from Minden, a rare and almost complete survival from the Middle Ages, shows the technique used in an ecclesiastical context, combined with plaques and golden ornaments, whilst the single mask and few acorns of pearls still in place on the Butler-Bowden cope show something of the original richness of these embroideries.

The incorporation of gold ornaments similarly enlivened the decoration, catching the light and adding an impressive three-dimensional quality. The ornaments, as with pearls, could simply be assembled and sewn into place and did not therefore demand the services of skilled embroiderers. Rather, they involved goldsmiths to create them in specially carved moulds, drawing these craftsmen into the large embroidery workshops. Also catching the light in embroideries were *doublets* – tiny discs of glass

47

of a type still seen in Indian embroideries — which appear to have come from Venice.

Countless similar examples are described in both the English and French royal accounts of the fourteenth century, none of which, sadly, have survived. For the Christmas and New Year festivities in 1393–4, two gloriously extravagant and light-hearted concoctions of this kind were created for Richard II: a white satin doublet embroidered in gold with orange trees on which hung one hundred silver-gilt oranges, and a *'hancelyn'* (believed to be a loose outer garment), also of white satin which was embroidered with leeches, water and rocks, and amongst which were placed fifteen silver-gilt mussels and fifteen silver-gilt whelks. How these must all have sparkled in the subdued lighting of the medieval royal halls. Late medieval taste was particularly attracted to light-reflecting ornaments on clothing and horse-harness where movement would produce a multitude of glinting reflections. Consequently gold and silver motifs of all shapes and sizes were incorporated into embroidery. In 1441 the Goldsmiths Company confirmed and renewed their *Ordinance for Making Spangles* which fixed prices. These 'spangles' were the equivalent of modern sequins, small, round, thin pieces of glittering metal with a hole in the centre to admit a thread; some were rectangular in shape and sewn at one end only, whilst others were rings of gold. Only a small quantity now survive *in situ* on embroideries but a number have turned up in archaeological contexts, perhaps the small lost hoards of people in flight from invaders.

53 The Annunciation worked on a mitre from Minden of *c.*1400 in silk, pearls and silver-gilt motifs; the scene on the reverse is the Virgin Enthroned.

Although there appears to have been a guild or confraternity of embroiderers in fourteenth-century London no statutes now survive. However, it has already been shown that many professional embroiderers were active in London, a number of whom, the Setteres and Heyrouns for example, lived in the area of the main east-west thoroughfare of Cheapside. We may surmise that the craft as a whole aimed at standards similar to those laid down in Paris in the late thirteenth century although, sadly, the few references to be found in City records show London embroiderers in a poor light. In 1369, for instance, a bill of complaint was brought against Elis Mympe, *brouderer*, of London, by John Catour of Reading whose daughter Alice had been apprenticed to Mympe for five years. Mympe, Catour alleged, had beaten and ill-treated Alice and had failed to provide for her. In 1385 a woman was accused of taking in a certain starving woman and others as apprentices in the craft of embroidery, whereas her real interest was to set up a house of infamy. All medieval

54 Young girls weaving, spinning and working upon embroidery, from *The Triumph of Minerva* frescoes of *c*.1470, by Cosimo Tura and Francesco Cossa. (See also title page.)

crafts had their wayward members, however, and it has to be said of embroiderers that they were not usually found amongst the violent and criminal elements in the City.

The names of male embroiderers tend to dominate later documents, misleading writers into thinking that women disappeared from the craft, but the records of the royal household in the fourteenth and fifteenth century reveal a great many working either directly for the king or in the special workshops of the royal armourers. Women monopolised certain crafts such as the making of silk and gold threads, silk and linen braids, laces (ties), cords and ribbons, but embroidery they had come to share with men, earning a lesser wage, as was usual at the time. The later statutes of the Paris guild drop the female form when referring to masters or apprentices, but here again both the statutes and other evidence show that whatever form organisation of the craft took, women were still key workers.

For some people, embroidery could be a profitable craft. The will of John de Cologne, armourer to Edward III for a large part of his reign, has not yet been located but the quantity of work he undertook for the King, a consistent daily wage of 12d. over many years, and the additional patronage he would attract from the King's immediate circle no doubt made him a wealthy man by the end of his life. He owned properties in Cornhill which he had licence to crenellate as early as 1337, and his wife Dulcisse served in the household of the King's young wife, Philippa of Hainault. By 1360 William Glendale had succeeded Cologne, and the last person to hold this office under Edward III was Thomas Carleton, from 1368 onwards Carleton was an alderman of the City of London in 1382 and again in 1388, during which year he died. His will, made in 1382, gives his trade as *brouderer* and shows him to have been a wealthy man, owning property and rich personal goods, as well as a shield of arms:

1388–9 Monday next after F of SS Perpetua and Felicitas
7 March

CARLETON, (Thomas), *'brouderer'* – To be buried in St John the Baptist's Chapel within the north gate of St Paul's. To the master of the Fraternity of St John the Baptist, London, with its four wardens, and their successors he leaves a rent charge on his tenements in the parish of St Alban in Wodstrete at the corner of Adelane, for the maintenance of a chantry in the aforesaid chapel; in default the said rent to go to the Mayor, Alderman, and Commonalty of the City for the same purpose. Bequests also of a vestment of blue silk, namely, a chasuble with white amice, stole, *phanon*, girdle together with two frontals, two curtains, two towels, a cushion for supporting a book, a chalice with *corporas* and cover, two cruets, a bell and a *paxbred* of silver to serve in the said chapel. Five marks to be expended upon a marble slab to put over his place of burial, having his shield of arms worked in *laton* in the middle of a cross and a record of the day of his decease. To Johanna his wife he leaves all his tenements, rents, etc., and a tenement called *'le lyon on the hope'* with shops, etc., in Wodestrete in the parish of St Alphege, for life, unless the same has to be sold to discharge his debts; remainder to Agnes his daughter in tail; remainder in trust for sale of pious and charitable uses. Bequests also to the churches of St Peter de Wodstrete in Chepe and St Alban in Wodstrete; to Emma his mother, William his brother, Marion his wife's sister, and others. To the aforesaid chantry he further leaves in reversion two books, viz. a bible [*unam bibletecam*] and a Legend of Saints. Dated 25 December, AD 1382.

The will of John Strousburgh, another London *'brouderer'* who died in the same year reveals little more about the private life and possessions of one of the craft: his 'tenements with dovecot, gardens, etc, upon Houndesdich in the parish of St Botolph without Algate' sound a pleasant inheritance for his daughter Alice and suggest that he had been successful. The will of Robert Ashcombe, senior, *'brouderer'*, dated 13 May 1416, states that he was to be buried in the chancel of the church of St Alban in Wodestrete. In 1394–8 Robert and William Sanston were *Broudatores Domini Regis* to Richard II, whilst he had already been prominent in 1376–7 when he was one of two *'brouderers'* representing their mystery on the City's Common Council. Stephen Vyne, another embroiderer to Richard II, is said to have been recommended to the King by that great patron and connoisseur the Duc de Berry. Wardrobe accounts of successive English kings reveal consistent patronage of London embroiderers, the office of King's Embroiderer always being held by a male. In 1441 Henry IV granted a commission to his *'broiderer'* John Mounshill to take 'needleworkers and broiderers, both men and women, necessary for the King's works and to superintend the said works for certain charges at the King's wages; also to take silk, thread, silver and gold of copper and solder, and to imprison all men and women who resist.'

After the fourteenth century the quality of English embroidery declined severely, the well-drawn designs degenerating into crude clumsiness, and the fine split-stitch giving place to a coarse satin-stitch. Nevertheless embroiderers attempted to maintain standards as before. In 1400–1, for example, men of the mystery complained that people occupying the craft were making 'divers werkes of Brouderie of unsuffisiaunt stuff, and unduely wrought as well upon velowt, and cloth of gold or silver of Cipre [Cyprus], and gold of Luk [Lucca], or Spaynyssh laton togedre', which goods they were sending out of London and were offering for sale at the fairs of Stourbridge, Ely, Oxford and Salisbury. During the fifteenth century the importation of foreign embroideries was more than once forbidden by statute to protect home production, for Flanders and Italy were outstripping the English and French embroiderers in both skill and design.

Formal contracts and details of commissions appear not to have survived in northern Europe, but documentation from fifteenth-century Italy throws light upon the background to several important commissions. In 1466 the Arte della Mercanzia, the Merchant's Guild of Florence, commissioned the artist Antonio Pollaiuolo 21 (*c*.1432–98) to design orphreys for a set of vestments for use at the principal feasts in the Baptistry of S. Giovanni; the theme of the orphreys was St John, patron saint of the 56 Baptistry. The account books of the Guild contain a series of entries between 1466 and 1480 relating to the commission, providing a picture of the progress of the work to completion and the names of those involved, including each of the eleven embroiderers. The first

55 Panel, originally from a cope, of brown velvet embroidered with a motif of the Virgin supported by angels surrounded by fleurs-de-lis and angel motifs worked separately in yellow silk and gilt metal thread. English work of the late fifteenth century.

56 St John preaching before Herod, after a design by Antonio Pollaiuolo, worked in Florence in the *or nué* technique.

embroiderers were noted on 5 August 1466: Coppino di Giovanni di Bramante from Malines, Piero de Venezia [Venice], Pagolo d'Anverza [Antwerp] and Jansicuro di Navarra. On 1 December Antonio di Giovanni of Florence, Gianpagolo da Perpignan and others were gradually drawn in to the group, including Paolo di Bartolommeo of Verona, an embroiderer celebrated in his own lifetime and recorded by Vasari; in 1477 the consuls granted him permission to 'make and embroider two portraits of the Pope', and in 1480 he went on to execute important embroideries for the Badia. Although Pollaiuolo must have drawn up designs before the embroiderers were commissioned in 1466, he was not mentioned until 9 August 1469 when it was recorded that 'the cartoons are being painted by Antonio di Jacopo da Pollaiuolo, for which 99 florins are being paid.'

The cartoons were executed in watercolour, and were so accurate and precise that when copied by a highly skilled embroiderer the effect was an impressive translation of the artist's intentions. Of the S. Giovanni pieces Vasari wrote that they 'were executed no less excellently with the needle than if they had been painted by Antonio with a brush; for which we are indebted in no small measure to the skill of the one in designing and the patience of the other in embroidering.' That other was, of course, 'Paolo da Verona, divine in that craft, and excelling every other master', again Vasari's opinion. The quality of the designs and workmanship on the embroideries vary quite considerably and it is believed that not all are the direct work of Antonio Pollaiuolo, but rather that of his younger brother Piero (c.1441–96), who seems to have supervised much of the work for his brother. The technique of or nué offered the best possible opportunity for the translation of a detailed cartoon, and clearly some of Paolo da Verona's fellow embroiderers did not achieve the same mastery of the technique. The work of each of the twenty-seven pieces is almost certainly that of a single craftsman, not of a group, the largest pieces being 51 × 30 cm. Just a hundred years later Vasari noted that this technique of needle-painting 'is almost lost, the custom in our day being to use larger stitches, which are less durable and less beautiful to see.'

It is probable that Pollaiuolo and the embroiderers in Florence had formal contracts of agreement with the Arte della Mercanzia not dissimilar to the contracts between embroiderers and the administrators of the tomb of St Anthony of Padua in 1478–84 when a set of vestments was given to the Basilica of S. Antonio by Pope Sixtus IV. These detailed contracts demonstrate the concern of both parties regarding agreement for all aspects of what was in fact purely a business matter. Four of these contracts now survive. The first, drawn up and signed on 19 January 1478, was made between Master Bernardo, embroiderer, and the administrators of the tomb of St Anthony, for the embroidery of the orphrey of a chasuble:

Master Bernardo, embroiderer, son of Leonardo of Milan, living in Venice, in the district of St Bartholomew, of his own accord etc. agrees with the noble master Archoano de Buzacharinis and master Pietro Mussato, citizens of Padua … to make fine orphreys for a chasuble. [He will do this] entirely at his own risk and expense, both regarding the gold and the silk [thread] and other things necessary [for this work]. [The orphreys should be] of the same quality and form as the design which is to be made by master Pietro Calzetta, here present, who has been unanimously chosen by the parties to this agreement. This design is to be made by the same master Pietro at the expense of master Bernardo. These orphreys are to be made with four figures on the back of the chasuble, three corresponding in length to a certain panel in the possession of master Bernardo, and the other should be of the length which is marked, and there should be a further figure on the rear corresponding in size to a figure on the Gattamelata chasuble … There should be three figures on the front, corresponding in length to another panel in the possession of master Bernardo, and two half-length figures, with the arms of Our Lord Pope Sixtus IV and the papal tiara beneath these half-length figures.

And the aforesaid orphreys may be made more rather than less beautiful than the sample given by the said master Bernardo to the representatives. And for the payment of the same master Bernardo for the aforementioned work the aforesaid representatives have promised to give the same master Bernardo two hundred gold ducats in three installments: that is to say a third two days after the next Feast of St Anthony, a third at the next Feast of the Nativity of Our Lord after that, and the balance at the Feast of St Anthony in the year 1479. With this [proviso] however, that the said master Bernardo

57 Detail from a chasuble, believed to be the only embroidery remaining from the vestments of Pope Sixtus IV, partly restored.

should give and hand over the completed orphreys to the same administrators before the eve of the Feast of St Anthony after next, in order that the orphreys can be placed on the chasuble and sewn, ready for the said eve.

A second contract, drawn up on 25 August 1478, shows the administrators commissioning orphreys for a cope and its hood, and, if these were well executed, borders and apparels of two dalmatics from another embroiderer with Milanese origins, Pietro da Pusterla. These embroideries were also to be designed by Pietro Calzetta, and were to be of the same quality as those already being worked by Master Bernardo. Unlike contemporary painters' contracts where concern centred upon quality of materials, these embroiderers' contracts show a great concern for quality of workmanship, the embroiderer being left to acquire the materials for his work. It is interesting, too, to note the way that the painter was effectively subcontracted to the embroiderer in these contracts, rather than directly employed by the patron, although he does seem to have been specifically chosen by both parties. Like Master Bernardo, Pietro da Pusterla was to be rewarded with the sum of two hundred ducats for his efforts, paid as he completed and handed over each section of the orphreys. On 31 December 1484 da Pusterla received a further commission from the administrators of the tomb, to make two stoles and three maniples to complete the set of vestments donated by the recently deceased Pope Sixtus IV.

In the contract already referred to between Master Bernardo Scudellino, embroiderer, and Jacopo, Bishop of Padua, on 2 May 1480, there is an interesting reference to a paper, by implication a paper pattern of the maniples in question: 'Item, that he should make the … maniples of the dalmatic and tunicle, of which there are four, two each, according to the size which is indicated on the paper so that each maniple has two figures each on the upper part, and should have some gold flowers on the lower part, with no figures'. The Bishop of Padua was a most demanding patron, for the contract stipulated, with reference to the making of an orphrey cross, that 'the faces should be good and well made, and that those which do not

please his lordship should be changed and made in a more pleasing manner'.

The embroiderers did not make up the vestments nor, indeed, even apply their work to them. Instead this appears to have been done by a tailor.

Almost none of the embroidered orphreys or apparels for vestments mentioned above have survived. A chasuble now in the Museo Antoniano at Padua bears the only embroidery to survive – a shield containing the Della Rovere oak tree, with the papal tiara and keys above it, 57 now placed at the rear of the chasuble, but originally on the front. The oak tree is executed in couched sequins on a ground of metallic thread couched with blue silk in the *or nué* technique, whilst the papal tiara is of mixed technique.

Despite the competition from Flanders and Italy the English and French embroiderers found sufficient work and continued to flourish. A political rhyme of the time of Edward IV (1461–83) suggests that Cheapside, the main thoroughfare of the City of London, still acted as a centre for embroiderers:

Erly in a someristide
y sawe in London, as y wente,
A gentilwoman of chepe-side
workinge on a vestment.

Their work still centred upon ecclesiastical vestments and court work, a number of officers of their Guild appearing in royal accounts and continuing the tradition of enriching royal garments. In their petition to Henry VII in 1495 the '*Brouderers*' spoke of those 'using the Craft within the City and suburbs' who 'wyrke any maner of broudered werke as flowers ymages or orfrays to be sette upon velwet satyne and damaske.' However, the embroideries that survive from the fifteenth century show how much the design and work of the craft had deteriorated. More often than not identical 55 motifs are scattered across the ground, mass-produced and lacking any imaginative concept. It is little wonder that it was to the Italian silk-weavers that Henry VII turned in 1500 for magnificent vestments.

58 Flemish cope hood, possibly depicting St Margaret and her dragon, in coloured silks and couched gold thread, with raised architectural ornament; probably early sixteenth century.

7 PATRONS

Embroidery is a time-consuming craft. As a domestic occupation in the Middle Ages its importance was directly related to the affluence of the household, and the majority of medieval women would have had little or no time for such luxuries in a life centering upon survival. From an early date, therefore, direct patronage of professional embroiderers was the only means of producing beautifully worked artefacts. The scant documentary evidence from the early Middle Ages reveals that there were women in the community with the special skills required to work with gold thread, indeed to make it, and shows how they were prized and rewarded by their patrons. No information survives about the size of the workforce gathered round these experts, but it is almost certain that it was not large.

Patronage was also important to help cover the costs of the materials, often as work progressed, although by the thirteenth century it is clear that merchants were well established as middlemen, anticipating demand and facilitating production. Greed and competition for these beautiful textile products knew no bounds. They not only stimulated an expansion in production, but filled Church treasuries, which became the main beneficiary, so far as we know, of the embroiderers' art in the Middle Ages, building up vast repositories later to be plundered so devastatingly.

For example, Pope Innocent IV was so impressed by some English ecclesiastical vestments that he requested they be sent to him. As Matthew Paris reported:

Then exclaimed the pope, 'England is for us surely a garden of delights, truly an inexhaustible well; and from there where so many things abound, many may be extorted. I hereupon, the same Lord Pope, allured by the desire of the eye, sent letters, blessed and sealed, to well nigh all the Abbots of the Cistercian order established in England, desiring that they should send to him without delay, these embroideries of gold which he preferred above all others, and with which he wished to decorate his chasubles and choral copes, as if these acquisitions would cost him nothing. This command of my Lord Pope did not displease the London merchants who traded in these embroideries and sold them at their own price.

The Pope knew that those seeking his influence or patronage were very likely to satisfy his craving, for embroidered vestments had long been important tools in international diplomacy.

This desire for rich embroidery continued and as we already know Gregory of London, a gold embroiderer, was residing in the papal household of Pope Urban IV (1261–4) generously supported by the Prior and Convent of Bermondsey. By 1295, the Vatican treasury could list 113 embroideries solely designated as English work, *opus anglicanum*, one of which must have been the cope for which Pope Nicholas IV thanked Edward I in 1291; in about 1295 Edward sent another to Pope Boniface VIII. Both of these popes presented copes of *opus anglicanum* to local cathedrals, and these still survive. Pope John XXII (1316–34) received several copes as gifts from England: two costly copes, one of them with large pearls, which were sent to him by Edward II and Queen Isabella on his accession, a precious cope sent by the Archbishop of Canterbury in 1322, and a sumptuously embroidered cope sent by the Bishop of Ely in 1333.

City of London records of this date reveal brief details of several transactions between patrons and embroiderers. For instance in 1307, Alexander le Settere came before the Mayor of London and received £10 from the chaplain of Master William Testa, Archdeacon of Lichfield and Coventry in part payment of £40 which the Archdeacon owed him for 'that embroidered choir cope of his, which he bought, and which the same Alexander will well and befittingly complete, of the same breadth around as a certain cord: the same to be delivered during the fortnight after Easter next.' In the same year a London embroidered cope was said to be worth £30, whilst in 1317 Rose de Burford, wife of a London merchant, was owed 100 marks (£66

59

59 The Ascoli Piceno Cope, given by Pope Nicholas IV (Girolamo Masci 1288–92) to his birthplace, Ascoli, in 1288. It is English work of *c*.1275–80 on a linen ground covered with scenes from the lives of the Popes from Clement I (90–100) to Clement IV (1265–8), embroidered in silk thread in split stitch and underside couched gold thread.

13s. 4d.) by Queen Isabella for an embroidered choir cope. In 1304, 300 marks (£200) was the price of a large cloth (approximately 9 m × 7.5 m) embroidered in gold and silk by Aleyse Darcy and sold to Henry de Lacy, Earl of Lincoln.

A patron of another kind was Odo, Bishop of Bayeux (1049/50–1097), who is now regarded as the instigator of that early and large embroidery known as the Bayeux Tapestry. Little is known of the origin of this work and many theories have therefore been advanced, most popular being the romantic but baseless story that it was worked by William the Conqueror's wife Matilda and her ladies for his half-brother Odo, Bishop of Bayeux. The emphasis given to Odo in the narrative would certainly point to him as a central personality in the creation of the embroidery, as he is not given the same importance in the historical chronicles. Today, it is believed that the embroidery was commissioned by Odo for use in a secular setting; that it was created within a generation of the events it depicts; that it was designed by an English artist, most likely a monk from or at Canterbury; and that the embroidery workshop may have been sited near Canterbury. The tradition that the embroidery was commissioned for display in Bayeux Cathedral has now been discounted. Its first documentary association with that Cathedral is in an inventory of 1476 which records that it was hung there in late June at the Feast of the Relics, but it is now believed that it was created purely for a secular purpose and its length of over 70.35 m means that originally it would have been better suited to a large hall in one of Odo's principal residences than to the Cathedral. There are a number of contemporary records of such narrative hangings ornamenting a large hall or chamber, reminding us of the considerable decorative importance of textiles as wall-hangings in the Middle Ages. It seems likely that we should envisage the narrow (0.5 m) tapestry hung at approximately eye-level around a large stone and wood medieval hall, with other hangings of embroidery or silk above it.

Many patrons liked to see their donations suitably inscribed so that all who viewed them

ET·HIC·EPISCOPVS·CIBV·ET·
POTV: BE NE DIC IT.

60 Bishop Odo (centre) and his half brother, Duke William of Normandy, feasting before the Battle of Hastings. Detail from the Bayeux Tapestry.

could be in no doubt about their source. An example is the large dark blue silk panel worked in silver and silver-gilt thread with the figure of Christ enthroned and the inscription JOHANNIS DE THANETO, probably originally part of a cope. An eighteenth-century antiquarian records that John of Thanet was a 'Monk and Chaunter' of Canterbury Cathedral, 'well-versed in the Mathematicks; but especially skilled in Musick. He set the Services and Offices for this Church, and wrote some Legends of Saints. He died in the year 1330 . . . being aged 92 years.' A cathedral inventory of 1316 also records an embroidered chasuble and alb associated with John of Thanet.

61

62 *Above* Detail of fig. 36 showing a kneeling figure, the female donor, to the left of the Adoration of the Magi.

61 *Opposite* 'John of Thanet' panel, 1300–20. The seated figure of Christ enthroned is 68.5 cm (2′ 3″) high, on a larger scale than any other example of English medieval embroidery.

63 Detail of Anna Malterer's arms from the Malterer Hanging.

Small kneeling figures representing the donors themselves are often found incorporated into the embroidered design, in just the same way as they appear in manuscript illuminations and panel-paintings of the time. A female donor 62 is depicted on an altar-cloth worked by Sophia, Hadewigis and Lucardis (nuns at the convent at Altenburg) which includes the kneeling figure of a monk, identified as Henricus de Cronenberg, who had relatives at the convent in the fourteenth century, one of whom was presumably the donor.

Patronage could be given a further visual boost by the incorporation of heraldic motifs in the embroidery, an attractive and compelling means of communicating individual generosity and social standing. Many sets of heraldic albs, stoles and maniples are recorded in medieval cathedral inventories, visibly demonstrating sources of benefaction. The heraldic orphreys on the Syon Cope were added when the original 16 chasuble was converted into a cope. They had been brought from other vestments: the orphrey round the circumference, for example, consists of the remains of a stole and maniple which, with the chasuble, had probably formed a set of matching Mass vestments. The arms throw little light on the origin of the vestments, however, and the basis on which they were selected remains uncertain. William de Clinton, 64 first Earl of Huntingdon, was a trusted friend of Edward III, and the remains of a cope orphrey incorporating his arms with those of his wife Juliana de Leybourne clearly indicate benefaction of vestments. He gave a cope and other vestments to St Albans Abbey, but it is not certain that these were they.

Independent embroidery workshops, devoted entirely to satisfying royal demands, were not peculiar to England and France. The magnificent mantles of Stephen of Hungary or 13 Roger II of Sicily can only have been produced 65 in this way and would have kept a group of skilled workers employed for several years. This kind of patronage meant not only that skills were exercised and presumably passed on to apprentices, but also that the demands made upon artists and embroiderers influenced and advanced the nature of the designs as well as of

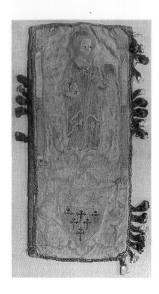

the techniques tackled. Something of the work and organisation of royal workshops has already been explained and this method of working appears to have continued through the later Middle Ages. The increasing use of embroidery in the secular sphere may also have affected its production for ecclesiastical purposes, whilst both were in turn affected by the growing quantities of decorative skills and velvets being produced in and exported from Italy and Spain. However, weaving could not yet produce the symbolic ornament so admired and necessary in northern courtly circles and so embroiderers continued to flourish, patronised by a growing and increasingly rich aristocracy intent upon the maintenance of status through visual display. Royal and noble houses gradually extended their own magnificence to their retinues, whose livery began to include embroidered badges which the king or duke himself wore in a more extended form.

Patronage might also come from the embroiderer's local community, one such example 56 being the set of orphreys dealing with the life of St John commissioned in 1466 from Antonio Pollaiuolo by the Merchants' Guild of Florence. According to Vasari, the embroidery took some twenty-three years to complete and the orphreys were mounted on specially woven white and gold silk.

A number of funeral palls or burying cloths of the late fifteenth to early sixteenth centuries still survive in London, the property of some of the major livery companies or trade guilds: the Merchant Taylors, the Brewers, the Saddlers, and the Fishmongers. These attractive cloths covered the coffin on the hearse and ensured that every member of the Company might expect a fitting burial, whatever his means. It is assumed that all these examples were commissioned from their fellow Londoners, the embroiderers. They all have a central panel of cloth of gold or velvet, whilst the side panels follow a similar layout, variously bearing religious motifs, the arms of the Company, and its patron saint. The pall of the Worshipful Company of 67 Brewers, dating from about 1500, has a central panel of Italian cloth of gold, and side panels of red velvet embroidered with the Assumption of

64 Shield of the arms of William de Clinton (*d.*1354), from fragmentary remains of a cope orphrey which also include the arms of his wife Juliana de Leybourne (*m.*1329, *d.*1367); they are worked in split stitch and couched work on buff silk damask. William de Clinton, first Earl of Huntingdon, was a close friend of Edward III and the recipient of painted and embroidered jousting equipment made in the London workshops of the King's armourers. It is likely that this cope was commissioned from London embroiderers.

65 Mantle of red silk twill ornamented with a bold design of a tree of life flanked by representations of a lion attacking a camel, worked in gold thread and coloured silks enhanced with pearls, gold ornaments, enamels and jewels. The mantle was made in the royal workshops in Sicily, probably for King Roger (1130–54), and later became part of the coronation insignia of the German kings and emperors. The Kufic inscription in Arabic round the hem records the year and place of manufacture.

the Virgin, the Company's arms, the seated figure of its patron saint, St Thomas of Canterbury, and his arms. The embroidery is typical of its time, couched gold thread with some split-stitch. Direct patronage of London embroiderers by affluent members of these large guilds is highly likely, although little information now survives.

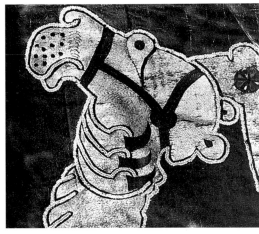

66 *Above* Detail of the head of the camel in fig.65, showing the packed rows of fine couched gold thread and the double row of tiny pearls forming the outlines.

67 Pall, or coffin cover, of the Worshipful Company of Brewers of 1490–1538.

EPILOGUE

Manual craftsmen such as embroiderers were rarely affected by changes of king or century and arbitrary time spans are usually irrelevant, since their contribution to society was a continuous process. Many changes in society were to influence and alter the work of the embroiderers in the Middle Ages, the greatest being the increasing use of embroidery for domestic purposes and the quantities of rich silks and velvets being exported from Italy and Spain.

The shortage of documentation outside the sphere of royal courts and noble households tends to obscure the expanding use of embroidered ornamentation in the later Middle Ages. The young wife of the Carpenter in Chaucer's *Canterbury Tales* − 'whyt was hir smok, and brouded al bifore' − was not altogether a fanciful creature of literature; she is in the same tradition as the knight in the slightly earlier poem *Sir Gawayne and the Grene Knight* whose gorgeous fighting gear was closely paralleled by the contemporary extravagances of the English and French kings and their knights. These ornate garments passed, at second, third and fourth hand, to succeeding generations through the lively second-hand market, whilst growing affluence − indeed, often considerable wealth − in the merchant sector raised expectations and increased the acquisition of these important status symbols.

Narrow borders of little more than decorative hemming on the edges of linen chemises gradually increased until by the end of the fifteenth century they had begun to emerge as fashionable features of dress. The skills to carry out such work were not great, being based on the quickly learned counted-thread stitches; many therefore could aspire to these small fashionable details. They spread rapidly, gradually became exaggerated and eventually emerged as the mid-sixteenth century ruff. Most women seem to have prepared their own underwear, so that to add small amounts of decorative needlework was natural if time were

no consideration. They would then go on to add this type of decoration to many other pieces of domestic linen, mainly bed-linen and towels. Towels were objects of ceremonial use, especially associated with handwashing during medieval feasts; they were of linen and examples with decorative woven borders survive. Women with greater ambitions would go on to tackle more extensive projects. The acceptability of embroidery as an occupation for noble ladies has an ancient history and it was customary to commence instruction when they were quite small. A treatise written in about 1300 by Walter de Biblesworth, tutor of the Kentish heiress Diane de Montchesney, described the way that a child, coiffed after supper, was to work in silk and thread, under instruction from her *tutresse*.

Samplers are known only from the early sixteenth century, although they must certainly have been worked for quite some time before this. They are a further manifestation of the rise of the amateur needlewoman and not all were worked by children. Some show an adult, even a professional, touch and documentary evidence indicates that originally the sampler was devised and used by adult needlewomen for a quite specific purpose. For instance at the beginning of the practice in the late fifteenth and early sixteenth centuries no printed patterns for needlework existed. It was an obvious expedient, therefore, for needlewomen to make, and exchange, embroidered memoranda of any interesting designs that came to their notice so they could refer to them later as required. When finished, the sampler was kept carefully and was even bequeathed by will. In great households, indeed, samplers seem to have been collected together into reference libraries: an inventory of Joan the Mad, Queen of Spain, dated 1509, lists no fewer than fifty samplers, some worked in silk, others in gold thread. The Privy Purse expenses of Elizabeth of York, consort of Henry VII, record in 1502 the taking of 'en elne [45 inches] of lynnen cloth for a sampler for the

68 *Above* The 'Fetternear Banner', a unique large embroidery in coloured silks on linen attributed to Scotland in about 1520; the border incorporates the arms of Gavin Douglas, Bishop of Dunkeld (1515−22).

69 *Opposite* Portrait of a man with a ring, 1505, by L. Beck. The sitter wears a highly fashionable ornate shirt with gold and pearl embroidery on the deeply gathered neck edge.

70 The front (*top*) and back (*above*) of a fifteenth-century German towel end with a needle-run border in green, blue, purple and black silk. The design is not regular, having many inaccuracies which suggest that it was worked without the aid of a chart. It imitates the towels with woven pattern ends which were produced earlier in Italy.

71 Unfinished German sampler worked in coloured silks on linen in cross, long-armed cross, two sided Italian cross and double running stitches. The crucifix was a fairly common motif in early sixteenth-century continental samplers; alphabets were less usual.

Quene' to Windsor. Thereafter the word begins to make more frequent appearances in dictionaries and literature. One of the earliest surviving samplers appears to relate to embroidery for 71 church linen; the motifs are in the style of the earliest group of pattern-books, about 1523–40.

It was natural that this interest in embroidery patterns would sooner or later be exploited commercially. Germany is believed to have been producing single pattern-sheets from the late fifteenth century onwards and was responsible for the first printed pattern-book, Johannes Schönsperger's *Ein New Modelbuch* (Zwickau 1524). This was followed rapidly by designs of similar books, issued chiefly from German and Italian presses. French publishers soon followed this lead, and England made a belated appearance in the field in 1587. These books include linear designs of the Holbein type, late Gothic floral ornaments, Renaissance strapwork, and many patterns for lacis and for counted-thread embroidery. The pattern-books came from centres of printing and of international trade rather than from areas important for embroidery, so that the earliest books were from Germany and it was a mere accident that Venice was a centre both for needlework and for the production of ephemeral illustrated books. Intended for the amateur embroideress, the books were conventional rather than novel, the earliest including patterns of late medieval design which only gradually gave way to Renaissance strapwork, 77 Moorish arabesques and grotesque ornaments based on the rediscovered 'antiques' of Ancient Rome. No technical innovations were suggested until the 1540s, when a series of Italian pattern-books was published which included designs clearly intended for cutwork.

These books are interesting in that they provide illustrations of embroiderers at work, albeit the affluent and industrious female clients of the booksellers. Some also include technical instructions. Alessandro Paganino's *Libro primo ... de rechami* of 1527, for example, shows women tracing embroidery designs onto cloth 29 already stretched on embroidery frames and includes a commentary on the ways this could be achieved; he certainly was aiming his publication at novices. The means of conveying the

72 'The Consecration of
St Augustine', a panel painting by
Jaime Huguet (c.1448?–1487)
from the retable of the Guild of
Tanners, Barcelona.

designs is also interesting to the modern
needlewoman, showing that little has changed
in over four hundred years. As well as bold line
drawings these pattern-books include finely
29 drawn square grids with solid squares indicating
a cross-stitch; some designs show stitches indicated by a dot in the square. The introduction
of printed books was to have considerable
repercussions for embroidery, as it did in so
many areas of life, and lead it away from the
accepted usages of the Middle Ages.

Earlier innovations in the production of fine silks
and velvets were also to have far-reaching
effects on professional embroidery as the Middle
Ages drew to a close. The Church's response to
secular fashions in textiles was partly influenced
by the fact that so many were donated to it and
there seems to have been no objection to the
conversion of secular garments with all manner
of ornamentation (squirrels, heraldic leopards
for example) into vestments to enhance services.
Plain grounds had served well to display the
religious subject-matter of the earlier Middle
Ages, but the quantities of patterned silks from
Italy and Spain which began to flood northern
Europe in the fourteenth century, coupled with
the effects of the Black Death and secular
demand, tended to depress the standard of
embroidery and it became concentrated in the
72 orphreys and cope hoods. The rich gold-enhan-
ced velvets of the fifteenth century simply
increased this tendency, for they contributed a
most sumptuous visual effect perfectly in keep-
ing with contemporary fashionable taste. The
embroiderers endeavoured to compete by sim-
plifying their techniques and adopting mass-
production methods. During the first half of the
fifteenth century they abandoned their traditional method of fixing gold threads by
underside couching and adopted the simpler and
quicker surface couching. They worked in-
55 numerable identical motifs, such as angels and
conventional flowers, which could be powdered
over plain grounds. So far had the art deteriorated that in about 1500 Henry VII commissioned vestments 'of cloth of gold tissue,
wrought with our badges of red roses and
portcullises' not from the embroiderers of Lon-

don, but from the weavers of Florence and
Lucca. Where great patrons lead so other
patronage follows.

The destruction of medieval embroidery was
often directly related to its beauty and value.
Thus removal of jewels and pearls began the
process of spoliation, but did not invariably lead
to immediate destruction: the Butler-Bowden 74
cope for example, is now lacking most of the
pearls which discreetly enriched the lion-masks,
acorns, stars, crowns and mitres. Removal of
gold ornaments or gold thread was more
damaging. In 1371–3, for example, the worn-
out chasubles and copes of the once-powerful
Archbishop Lanfranc (c.1005–89) at Canterbury
Cathedral were reduced to ashes for the sake of
the gold in the embroidery, a practical and
economic process which should not surprise us.
Entries in the treasurer's accounts of Westminster Abbey for 1571 reveal rather more of this
process:

To Mr Greme goldsmyth for a sylver pott parcell guylt
prepared for the Comunyon waing li. oz. at vi s. [51 oz. at
6s.] le oz. the summe of xv li. vjs. [£15 6s.]. Towards wch

73 Fragmentary embroidery associated with the Florentine Geri Lapi. The background, stripped of most of the couched gold thread, reveals the thick cotton thread used to give a subtle third dimension to the setting of this dramatic scene of Christ with Mary Magdalene.

charge ther went xxxiiijor iii grts [34¾] of sylver that cam of the bur[n]ing of certen coapes at vs. [5s.] the oz. amounting to viij li. xiijs. ixd. [£8 13s. 9d.]

To the goldsmyth in regard for burnying the said coapes etc. vjs. viijd. [6s. 8d.]

Another entry in the same set of accounts reveals the fate of other copes from this rich treasury:

Thome Holmes upholster for thaltering of certain coapes into Quisshions Chaires etc. and for the workmanship and stuffe therunto as apperith by a bill – xj li. viij sh. vijd. [£11 8s. 7d.]

Many surviving medieval embroideries show signs of re-use when fashion or damage required it: the Syon Cope, for example, altered from a chasuble to a cope and given orphreys which were once a stole and maniple; the Clare

75 Mantle, the so-called 'Star-mantle', of the Emperor Henry II, originally of dark violet silk twill worked in couched gold thread with scenes from the Life of Christ, together with symbols of the heavenly bodies. The mantle was given to the Emperor by Duke Ismahel of Bari (*d.*1020) and was probably given to Bamberg Cathedral by Henry II or his wife St Kunigund. Probably south German work of about 1010–20.

76 Detail of 'Hercules and the Lernaean Hydra' from the 'Star-mantle' of the Emperor Henry II.

74 *Opposite* Detail from the upper register of the Butler-Bowden Cope of 1330–40 showing tiny pearls enriching the lion-masks and acorns of the architectural tracery.

Chasuble severely cut down in the post-medi-30 eval period; or the heraldic fragment, now a seal-bag.

The preponderance of embroideries for ecclesiastical use which survive attests the care and respect they have been accorded over the centuries. Embroideries for domestic or ceremonial use have suffered considerably through normal wear and tear, changes in fashions, and the very extensive recycling of textiles in the secular sector. When not worn out during the lifetime of their first owner, social custom frequently took a hand in their next manifestation. For instance, the will of Queen Matilda (d.1083), consort of William the Conqueror, states 'I give to the Abbey of the Holy Trinity [at Caen, founded by herself] my tunic, worked at Winchester by Alderet's wife, and the mantle embroidered with gold, which is in my chamber, to make a cope. Of my two golden girdles, I give that which is ornamented with emblems for the purpose of suspending the lamp before the great altar'; that of Sir Ralph Verney the

younger, proved in 1525, makes an almost identical disposal, 'I will that the gownes of dame Anne Verney late my wife, doo make vestiments to be given to Churches, according to the discrecion of myne Executors.' Edward III and his wife Philippa of Hainault may have presented most of their magnificent ceremonial robes to religious foundations or court favourites. We know that Queen Philippa's squirrel robe of 1330 went to Ely Cathedral in 1332/3 where it was turned into three copes for John Crauden, Prior of Ely (1321–4); the vestments made out of it survived to the Reformation. Shortly afterwards Edward III is believed to have presented richly embroidered heraldic horse-trapper (coverings) to a continental religious foundation. The heraldic jupon which was set up in 1376 over the tomb of their son the Black Prince in Canterbury Cathedral still survives although almost totally destroyed by the process.

25, 26

Wars, vermin and sheer old age have destroyed a vast quantity of medieval embroidery. In England widespread destruction of ecclesiastical work came about as the result of Henry VIII's conflict with the Church of Rome and his subsequent reformation of the Church of England. Contemporary inventories of just over a hundred churches and chantries in the City of London alone make sad reading as the destruction and dispersal of centuries of accumulated treasures began. Many vestments and hangings were purchased by City embroiderers, tailors, bed-makers and purse-makers, presumably to be re-used in the time-honoured tradition. St Botolph, Aldgate, sold various vestments to Harry Vaggon, broiderer, including one 'of red branched velvet with flowers of gold, stole, and fanon, £1 5s. 4d.', whilst the many sold to Robert Donkin, tailor, included a 'vestment of white damask with crowned Emmes [M' s], £1 0s. 5d.'. Those sold by St Bride's, Fleet Street, show the way in which magnificent sets of vestments were broken up:

Item solde more to Chrystofe Dray a Cope and the Deacon of blewe damaske with Eagles of Golde embrowdered and standyng upon mountayns for xiijs. iiijd. [13s. 4d.]. Item solde to the seid Mr Cordmaker [John Taylor, Vicar at St Bride's, subsequently burned at Smithfield] another Cope and the Chesabell of the same suyte for

xiiis. iiijd. Item solde to George Brodes the iijde. Cope and subdeacon of the same suyte for xiiis. iiijd.

From St Dionis Backchurch John Waterskot, goldsmith, purchased for 20s. 8d. 'iiij ouncys iij quarters sylver that cam of vestment that was burnte', and indeed many of the entries reveal vestments that had little chance of survival: ragged, rotten, 'sor brokyn', 'eaten with Rattes', or 'ful of holes' speak of neglect, decay and the inevitability of eventual destruction. More painful to read are the descriptions of the beautiful embroideries in St Paul's Cathedral which, in 1552, included three hundred copes alone. Some, like the 'grate large coope of nedell worke with divas ymages ther uppon' or the 'faire large coope of needleworke full of ymages with perles in the orpher' are very likely to have been the products of the nearby London embroiderers' workshops so sought after in the thirteenth and fourteenth centuries, whilst four 'goodlie newe coopes of whyght damaske with lillie pottes and the splayde Egle of the Kynges gifte' were clearly recent additions. The inventory of St Nicholas Cole Abbey records many embroidered orphreys, again presumably London work: the Birth of Our Lord, a crucifix with Mary and John, 'Gabriel, our Lady and Saynte Myghell', the Assumption of Our Lady, Christ on the Cross. No less than eighteen of these inventories include vestments ornamented with garters, revealing the resting place of so many of the early robes presented to knights of the Order, the garters mass-produced in the London workshops of a succession of King's Embroiderers. The flooding of the London market with these textiles, often at very advantageous prices, cannot help but have raised the material standard of living of a fair proportion of its citizens: grocers, pewterers, brewers, painters and foreign merchants are amongst those known to have benefited by the dispersal of vestments. A number of copes from Lilleshall Priory were turned into cushion covers for use in Hardwick Hall and the unused fragments stored away. It has been suggested that this sudden availability of such large quantities of embroideries on the market created a new taste and demand for these luxuries – perhaps, ironically, swelling the embroiderers' order books. Ironically, too, of the large collection of new vestments commissioned by Henry VIII's father, Henry VII, in 1500–2 from Italian weavers and bequeathed by him in 1509 to Westminster Abbey, only eleven copes remained in the Abbey by 1608, and these were burned by Puritans in 1643. Luckily some of the vestments, including one of the copes, were removed from the Abbey before 1608, taken abroad, and survived.

The Bayeux Tapestry, with its open reference to the French nobility and the English monarchy, should have been a prime candidate for destruction in 1792 when the Revolutionary Government of France declared that all works of art and all documents which reflected the history or 'vanity' of the monarchy were to be destroyed by the people. However, it remained forgotten in its storage place in Bayeux Cathedral, generally unknown outside antiquarian and academic circles – until the day, that is, when the local contingent of Bayeux was called up to serve in the Franco-Prussian War. One of its wagons needed a protective cover and, such was contemporary local sentiment that the Tapestry was pressed into service but, by providing a satisfactory substitute, the local Commissary of Police managed to save it. Still, some regarded it as a fairly worthless piece of cloth, suitable only for any immediate use, and in 1794 the Art Commission for Bayeux district recorded how it managed to prevent the Tapestry from being cut into strips to decorate a float for the Goddess of Reason during a local public holiday. Threats to historic embroideries continue to the present day and it is an unhappy fact that many fine ecclesiastical embroideries still languish in churches which are unable to pay for conservation or protective display facilities.

77 Page from Alessandro Paganino's *Libro primo ... de rechami* showing contemporary border designs coupled with a more archaic trapping scene.

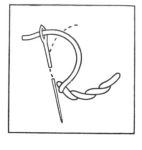

Stem stitch

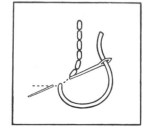

Back stitch

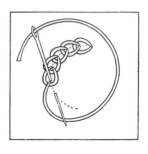

Chain stitch

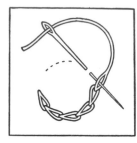

Split stitch

Satin stitch

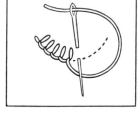

Buttonhole stitch

Cross stitch

Couching stitch

GLOSSARY

alb Enveloping white linen tunic worn by priests, sometimes under other vestments; often ornamented with apparels (q.v.) at cuffs and lower hem.

apparel Decorative panel, often embroidered, applied to albs, amices and other vestments.

chapel Matching set of ecclesiastical vestments.

chasuble Principal vestment worn by the priest for the celebration of the Mass.

cope Principal vestment worn for various church ceremonies; a semi-circular cloak, fastened across the chest by a brooch or strip of material (*morse*). The front edges were often adorned with orphreys (q.v.) and at the back of the neck is a vestigial hood.

counterpoint Quilted cover for a bed: a counterpane.

cutwork Decorative technique, usually on linen, in which both warp and weft are in places cut away, and the open spaces thus formed are partly refilled with decorative needleworked motifs.

dalmatic Shin-length, sleeved tunic worn by deacons assisting the priest at the Mass.

diaper ground Patterned area created by crossing diagonal lines which form diamonds.

drawn-work Decorative technique, usually on linen, in which the threads of either the warp or the weft of the material were withdrawn and those remaining worked into a pattern, by either clustering together or working over them in some fashion.

ell Old measure of length varying in different countries; the English ell equalled 1.14 m (45″).

fanon Maniple (q.v.)

Great Wardrobe Section of the English medieval royal household dealing with clothing and textile furnishings; they also dealt in all bulky dry goods such as rice, dried fruit, nuts, sugar, spices, candles, etc.

journeyman One who, having served his apprenticeship to a handicraft or trade, was qualified to work at it for days' wages.

knop A knob, boss, stud, button, tassel.

lacis Ancient technique in which hand-made knotted net is decorated with embroidery.

laton Latten, a mixed metal of yellow colour, either identical with or very like brass.

maniple Narrow strip of material worn over the left forearm by priest, deacon and sub-deacon.

mantlelet In medieval contexts an heraldic drapery featuring as

part of room- or bed-hangings, or used to ornament a tent; later an heraldic term.

mercer Dealer in silks and other costly materials.

mitre Cap with two points, or horns, worn by bishops and some abbots. From the back hang two narrow strips of material, called lappets.

opus anglicanum 'English work', a medieval term referring generally to fine ecclesiastical embroidery, believed especially to refer to that worked in the underside couching technique.

opus consutum Probably appliqué work (q.v.).

opus teutonicum Believed to refer to linen embroidery on linen (i.e. whitework).

orphrey Decorative band, often embroidered, used on chasuble, cope, dalmatic, etc. According to its shape and position it may

be termed a pillar-orphrey or cross-orphrey.

pall Textile covering for the coffin of the deceased during funeral ceremonies.

pulled thread work Warp and weft threads deliberately distorted by needlework stitches to create a decorative effect.

robe Set of three, four, five or six matching garments including tunics, mantles or cloaks.

silkwoman Specialist in spinning and dyeing silk, using it to plait or weave laces, braids and ribbons.

stole Narrow strip of material worn over the shoulders, by priests and deacons, and falling to the knee or lower.

sub-deacon See tunicle.

tunicle Shin-length, sleeved tunic similar, and sometimes identical to the dalmatic (q.v.), worn by sub-deacons.

FURTHER READING

ARTS COUNCIL,
Opus Anglicanum: English Medieval Embroidery, Exhibition catalogue, 1963.

S. A. BROWN,
The Bayeux Tapestry, Woodbridge, 1988.

MRS A. G. I. CHRISTIE,
English Medieval Embroidery, Oxford University Press, 1938.

MARGARET HARRINGTON DANIELS,
'Early Books for Lace and Embroidery', in *Needle and Bobbin Club*, 17, nos 1 & 2, New York, 1933.

JOAN EVANS,
Dress in Medieval France, Oxford University Press, 1952.

SANTINA LEVEY,
Lace, A History, London, 1983.

ARTHUR LOTZ,
Bibliographie der Modelbücher, Leipzig, 1933, 2nd edn 1963.

S. M. NEWTON,
Fashion in the Age of the Black Prince, Woodbridge, 1980.

ROZSIKA PARKER,
The Subversive Stitch, London, 1984.

M. SCHUETTE and S. MÜLLER-CHRISTENSEN,
The Art of Embroidery, London, 1964.

ANNE SEBBA,
Samplers: Five Centuries of a Gentle Craft, London, 1979.

MARGARET SWAIN,
Figures on Fabric, London, 1980.

DAVID WILSON,
The Bayeux Tapestry, London, 1985.

ACKNOWLEDGEMENTS

I am especially grateful to Donald King and Frances Pritchard for reading my draft and making helpful comments, to Philip Bennett for smoothing out translation problems, and to Philippa Glanville, Lisa Monnas and Naomi Tarrant for support and suggestions.

Karen Finch and Hélène Lander clarified technical details, whilst a grant from the Raine Fund of the Pasold Research Fund enabled me to locate additional documentary information as the by-product of another research project. For showing me examples in their collections I am grateful to John Cherry and Hero Granger-Taylor (British Museum), Linda Woolley (Victoria and Albert Museum), Milton Sonday and Gillian Moss (Cooper-Hewitt Museum, New York), Barbara Boehn and Nobuko Kajitani (Metropolitan Museum of Art, New York), Margareta Nockert (State Historical Museum, Stockholm), Dr Angela Völker and Blanda Winter (Austrian Decorative Arts Museum, Vienna).

Finally, for their great good humour and tolerance I thank my secretary Marion R. Williams and my editor Rachel Rogers.

INDEX

Page numbers in *italic* refer to the illustrations.

accounts 22, 27, 48
Aelfgyd 8
Aelgifu of Northampton 7
Aelgiva, Queen 8
Aethelswitha 8
altarcloths 7, 9, 37, *37*, 38, 59
altar frontal 9, 12, *20*, 35, 70
altar hangings 8, *38*
Anglo-Saxon 4, 18, 45
appliqué 29, 33ff.
apprentice 14, 15
armourer 22, 23, 27, 28, 46
artists 20, 21, 22
Ascoli Piceno Cope, *see* copes
Ashcombe, Robert 16, 50

banners 10, 21
Basing, Adam de 10, 12
Bayeux Tapestry 4, 27, 35, 40, 41, 57, *58*, 69

bed-hangings 6, 15, 21, 22, 30
bed-linen 62
Berry, Duc de 50
Black Prince, *see* Edward, the Black Prince
Bologna Cope, *see* copes
Bronze Age 4
Brouderer's Company 50
Burgundy 6
Butler-Bowden cope, *see* copes

Calzetta, Pietro 53
Canterbury Cathedral 33, 34
Canterbury Tales 62
Canute, King of Norway, Denmark and England 7, 8
Carleton, Thomas 49, 50
Cennini, Cennino 23, 24, 29, 31
chasubles 8, 9, 10, *15*, 18, *34*, 53, *53*, 66, 67, 70
Cheapside 49, 53
Chevalier, Estienne 14, 15
Chidelee, John de 23
Clinton, William de 59
clothing, embroidered 23, 27, 30
Cologne, John de 28, 30, 47, 49
contracts 52, 53
convents 8, 38, 42, 59
copes 8, 9, 18, 53, 55, 65, 66, 68, 70
  Ascoli Piceno Cope 56
  Bologna Cope *11*
  Butler-Bowden Cope 47, 65, 67
  Pienza Cope *contents page*, *26*
  Syon Cope 21, 59, 66
couched work *19*, 21, 29, 40ff., *45*, *60*, 61, 65
Cronenberg, Henricus de 59
cushions 9, *37*
Cuthbert, Saint 8, *8*

Darcy, Aleyse 57
Denmark 4, *4*, 5
designers 18, 19ff., *24*, *44*
Domesday Survey 8
donors 20, *20*, 41, 59
doublets (tiny glass discs) 47
Dragon, Order of the *31*
drawn-work 36, 70
Dunstan, Saint 19

Edith, Queen 8
Edward I, King of England 34, 55
Edward II, King of England 12, 55
Edward III, King of England 12, 23, 24, 28, 29, 30, 46, 49, 59, 68
Edward IV, King of England 53
Edward, the Black Prince, Prince of Wales 23, 68
Eleanor of Castile 7
Ely, Thomas of 7, 8
Etheldreda, Saint 7

flags 30
Flanders 24, 44, 53
Flémalle, Master of 25, *44*
fleurs-de-lis 29, 30, *40*, *51*
Florence 5, 20, 23, 24, 50, 60
folk-embroidery 34

frames (stretchers) 27, 28, 32
funeral pall 60

garters 23
Garter, Order of the 23, 30, 68
Germany 9, 34, 36, 38, 40, 41, 64
Glendale, William 49
gold 6, *8*, 42ff.
Golden Fleece, Order of the *18*, 24, 44, 45
goldsmiths 47, 48, 68
Great Wardrobe 28, 70
Gregory of London 55
guilds Chapter 2 *passim*

Halley, Nicholas 16
Hardwick Hall 68
Henry III, King of England 10, 12
Henry IV, King of England 16, 50
Henry V, King of England 20
Henry VII, King of England 53, 59, 65
Henry VIII, King of England 68
heraldry 21, 22, 25, 29, 30, 33, 59, 68
Heyroun family 49
Heyroun, Johanna 12
Heyroun, John 12
Holy Roman Empire 10, 24, 31, 46
hoods 47
horse-coverings 21, 22, *22*, 29, 30
Hungary 15, *19*, 31, 59

Iceland 41
Innocent IV, Pope (1243–54) 10, 55
inspectors 16
Iron Age 4
Italy 5, 20, 36, 44, 50, 53, 64

John XXII, Pope (1316–34) 55
John of Thanet 59
journeyman 14, 15, 70

Kerdyff, John de 23
King's Armourer 22, 23, 27, 28, 46
King's Embroiderer 21, 30, 50

Lapo, Geri di 20, 66
leopards 29, *29*, 30, 34
Lilleshall Priory 68
linen 41
London 4, 10, 13, 16, 21, 24, 27, 49, 53, 68
London, Gregory of 55

Mable of Bury St Edmunds 10
maniple 59, 70
mantles 9, 31, 44, 45, 60, 67
manuscript illuminators 20
Matilda, Queen 8, 57, 67
Maud de Benelieve 10
Maud de Cantuaria 10
mercers 18, 70
merchants 55
mitres 9, *9*, 47, 48
Mounshill (Mounselle), John 16, 50
Mympe, Ellis 49

Nicholas IV, Pope (1288–92) 55
night working 13, 15

opus anglicanum 10, 20, 21, 22, 27, 33, 35, 55, 70
opus consutum 34, 70
opus teutonicum 36, 70
or nué (shaded gold) 44, *51, 52*
orphreys 9, *21, 26, 31, 60, 65,* 70

Padua 52, 53
Paganino, Alessandro 31, *32, 64, 64*
painters 23
pall 60, *61,* 70
Paris 13, 15, 16, 18, 27
Paris, Matthew 10, 12, 55
pattern-books 53, 64, 65
patterns 29, 53
patrons 10, 21, 55ff., 60
pearls 46, *46,* 48, *61, 62, 67*
Philip (the Good), Duke of Burgundy 24, 45
Philippa of Hainault 23, 28, 49, 68
Pienza Cope, *see* copes
Pollaiuolo, Antonio 24, *25,* 50, *51, 52,* 60
purses 9, *43*
Pusterla, Pietro da 53

quilting 38ff., *38, 39, 40*

regulations 13, 18
Richard II, King of England 16, 30, 48, 50

samplers 62, *64*
Sanston, William and Robert 50
Scandinavia 34, 41
Scudellino, Master Bernardo 52, 53
seal bags *33, 34, 34, 36*
Settere family 49
Settere, Alexander le 12, 55
Settere, Matilda la 12
Settere, William le 12
Sewale, John 16
Sicily 38, 59, *60*
Sir Gawayne and the Grene Knight 62
Sixtus IV, Pope (1471–84) 52, *53*
sketchbook, Pepysian 24, *25*
Spain 36, 41, *41*
spangles 48
St Nicholas Cole Abbey 68
St Paul's Cathedral 68
stamping and stencilling silk 22
stitch
    back 40
    brick *38*
    chain 35, *41, 43*
    cross *21,* 36, *36*
    couching *41*
    filling 34ff.
    outline 34ff.
    plait *21*
    satin *41,* 50
    split *15, 21, 35, 35, 36, 43,* 50, *60*
    stem *5,* 34, 35, *41, 43*
stoles *8,* 59, 70
Strousburgh, John 30, 50
Strowesburgh, Hans de 30
Switzerland 36, 41
Syon Cope, *see* copes

tailors 27, 28, 53
techniques 33
theatrical costumes 21
thread
    cotton 44, *66*
    counted 62, 64
    counting 36ff.
    gold *15, 16, 18, 19, 20, 23, 29, 31, 32,* 40, *42, 43, 45, 58, 61*
    silk *21,* 28, *29, 32, 34, 42, 43*
    silver *21, 45*
towels 62, *63*
trestles 7
Tristan 7, *17,* 34, 38, *38*
tunic 28, 29, 30, 53
tunicle 18, 70

underside couching *8, 9, 15, 21,* 45ff.
Urban IV, Pope (1261–4) 12, 55

valet, see journeyman
Vasari, Giorgio 24, 52, 60
Vatican 55
veils 37
velvet 24, 28, 30, *51*
Venice 64
Verona, Paoloda 52
Viking 4
Villant, Pierre de 26

wages 9, 28, 49
wall hangings *8, 9, 15, 21,* 22, *41*
wax 28, 33
Westminster Abbey 9, 12, 21, 34, 65, 69
Weyden, Rogier van der 25, *44*
William the Conqueror 8, 57
William of Malmesbury 7
wool 41